On Defining Freud's Discourse

On Defining Freud's Discourse

PATRICK J. MAHONY

Yale University Press

New Haven and London

Designed by James J. Johnson and set in Linotype Walbaum types by The Composing Room of Michigan, Grand Rapids, Michigan 49501. Printed in the United States of America by BookCrafters, Inc., Chelsea, Michigan.

Library of Congress Cataloging-in-Publication Data
Mahony, Patrick, 1932–
    On defining Freud's discourse.
Bibliography: p.
    Includes index.
    1. Psychoanalysis—Case studies.   2. Freud,
Sigmund, 1865–1939—language.   I. Title.
[DNLM: 1. Freud, Sigmund, 1865–1939.   2. Psychoana-
lysis—biography.   3. Writing—biography.
WZ   100   F889MAA]
RC509.8.M345   1989   150.19'52   88–27699
ISBN 0-300-04347-3 (alk. paper)

The paper in this book meets the guidelines for permanence and durability of the Committee on Production Guidelines for Book Longevity of the Council on Library Resources.

10   9   8   7   6   5   4   3   2   1

To Pierrette,
our children,
and those dearly abiding in us

Ego proinde fateor me ex eorum numero esse conari, qui proficiendo scribunt et scribendo proficiunt.

Admittedly, therefore, I try to be among the number of those who write as they progress and who progress as they write.

—St. Augustine, letter 143
(my translation)

Contents

Acknowledgments

I am pleased that this is my third publication with Yale University Press. Its staff and readers continue to be helpful both in giving positive suggestions and in bringing attention to my mistakes; Stef Jones deserves special thanks for her perceptive comments. Way above and beyond the call of duty, Gladys Topkis repeatedly examined my manuscript and made it considerably better each time; I feel privileged to have her as senior editor and as a wonderful friend. I renew my gratitude to Darius Ornston for his treasured judgment of this as of my other works. As only she can do, Pierrette gave me an indispensable combination of support, inspiration, and alert commentary. Only at the end did I realize how much I had been helped and how much more I had been personally involved with this work than with my previous ones.

Introduction

In titling my book *On Defining Freud's Discourse*, I have followed the spirit of Freud's own expository endeavors. Again and again, the fragmentary and ongoing analysis recurrent in his work is better suggested in the modest nuance of the German titles. Thus, "Über den Gegensinn der Urworte" (1910) is literally "On the antithetical meaning of primal words" and *Zur Psychopathologie des Alltagslebens* (1910) must be rendered as "On the psychopathology of everyday life." In his translations Strachey suppressed the "on" and thereby eliminated Freud's tentativeness. One final example is even more telling. "New Introductory Lectures on Psychoanalysis" (1933), Strachey's title, undercuts the probing note of "Neue Folge der Vorlesungen zur Einführung in die Psychoanalyse," better translated as "A New Series of Lectures for the Introduction to Psychoanalysis."

If tentativeness is to be recognized as a prominent trait in Freud's prose, it should be seen an integral expressive part of his verbal powers. We must not be misled by the fact that the sole award Freud won during his lifetime was the Goethe Prize for Literature. Freud is one of the great masters of German prose, but if we admire his writing simply on aesthetic grounds, our appreciation is superficial. For a fuller understanding we might do better by pursuing the appraisal made by Einstein in a laudatory letter to Freud: "I do not know any contemporary who has presented his subject in the German language in such a masterly way." How, we might ask, is such a masterly exposition about the unconscious attuned to the unconscious of both Freud and his readers? I shall grapple with this question in the course of this book, and its answers will be successively clarified and augmented into an ever-broadening synthesis.

All three chapters of the book examine their material in the sequence of context and text. A discussion of historical background, restricted and tailored to my immediate purpose, will lead to an analysis of Freud's discourse proper. Chapter 1 serves as a general introduction to our subject. In chapters 2–3, I undertake a texual analysis of a pair of Freud's works, the case history of Katharina (1893–95) and "Analysis Terminable and Interminable" (1937). There are both intrinsic and extrinsic strategic reasons for my choice of these specimen texts: with nearly a half century between the times of their composition, they constitute more or less the termini of Freud's psychoanalytic career; they have recently been the object of renewed critical interest; more important, the two clinical works are of exceptional inherent value, the one being the most charming of Freud's case histories, the other possibly Freud's greatest technical contribution (Jones 1953–57, 3:250). Most important, they represent the dynamic extremes of Freud's most interesting kind of discursive practice.

Some further preliminary detail might prove helpful. In chapter 1 we have the chance to discover some of the fascinating historical background of Freud's two major discursive procedures, one which he called dogmatic, the other, genetic. It is in the quintessential genetic writing that Freud truly shows his daring. Here Freud opts for exploratory writing: rather than report an earlier exploration, he writes in order to find out what he is thinking and in turn shares that rich adventure with the reader. It is precisely this feature of his discourse that brings us back again and again to Freud's writings, even those containing findings that he subsequently disavowed. In the true genetic discourse, we meet with Freud's unconscious and with the psychoanalytic process. Not only does it involve a style used to write about psychoanalysis; it also manifests itself in a style that embodies the psychoanalytic experience. For that reason, Freud's style remains perennially fresh, more lively and engaging than many subsequent psychoanalytic treatises. In spite of their up-to-date contents, these later works are vapid in expression and hence short-lived, so that once their contents are surpassed by new observations, they are likely no longer to be read except by historical scholars.

Although Freud preferred a genetic method of writing, he was apt to combine it in various ways with the dogmatic. Such a combination is found in this book's two specimen texts, which, beside being exceptional in their own right, are valuable as complements to each other. The reader familiar with my previous publications (Mahony 1986, 1987) knows that I stress the indispensability of reading

Freud's texts in German, and to that effect I again call attention here to the shortcomings of translation found in Strachey's nevertheless admirable and monumental edition of Freud.

The case history of Katharina is actually the report of a single meeting—a fortuitous encounter that the vacationing Freud had on an Austrian mountaintop. If Katharina's case history is Freud's shortest, it is yet recognized as one of the most endearing pieces of writing he left us. Undoubtedly its charm was influenced by the evident sympathy Freud had for the traumatized young girl—she had already suffered too much; benevolent understanding is called for, and the reader's complete alliance and sympathy are taken for granted. To produce an atmosphere of unity in the text, Freud avoids his habitual practice of contending with authorities of various theoretical and clinical points of view. And apart from Katharina's abusive father, the only villain in the piece is the uncooperative, prudish lady of Freud's city practice, who holds whatever is natural to be turpid. Still, our textual inspection will show that interlocked with Freud's sincere concern was his own unsettlement, relived in the intriguing contours of his composition.

In many respects chapter 3 is the most important part of this book. The contrast between Katharina's case history and "Analysis Terminable and Interminable" is striking— a family tragedy gives way to the castastrophe of whole peoples, and an optimism about the lasting effects of a single interview dramatically yield place (though not completely) to a pessimistic judgment about the unendingness of analysis. We might expect Freud's culminative review of psychoanalytic practice to be set fort in a predominantly dogmatic discourse here; instead, we are greeted with a fascinating form of expression, loosely logical and distinguished by a highly creative use of language. In an exemplary gesture, Freud courageously enlisted this creative power to express his preoccupation with the future of humankind. (Why, apart from being brutalized by his own body, he needed so much courage should bring home to us the grief of this century of savagery, incredible, fully inexpressible, awful, yet necessary to be remembered.) Freud's late essay, a majestic scriptive enactment of his exceptional intellect and moral courage, is one of the foremost among his writings, and even one of the finest pieces of authorial commitment in our time. Thus Freud, amid his darkening moments, took pains to legate a hope, however flickering, for a mad, bellicose world, a world soon to become incomprehensibly madder in that its furnaces, once conceived to comfort people from the elements, would next be used to reduce them to them.

Let us now retrace Freud's path, from his early contact with his legendary teachers to his efforts as a novice analyst and analyst-writer, and then to his octogenarian concerns and retrospections on his followers and numerous patients—a long story of history and private experience wound into momentous record, a writing waiting always to be better known.

1

An Overview of Freud's Discourse

I invite you to travel with me thousands of miles away and decades back in time. As the picture gradually clears, we are in Vienna . . . in Berggasse 19 . . . in Freud's study . . . peering over his shoulder. It is November 1899, and the greatest book in the history of psychoanalysis is about to appear in print. Freud sits at his desk, answering a request that he supply a professional sketch of himself for the *Biographisches Lexikon hervorragender Ärtze des neunzehnten Jahrhunderts* (Biographical lexicon of eminent doctors of the nineteenth century), edited by Julius Pagel. In his autobiographical description Freud is at the point of naming his mentors. We strain closer as he twice designates himself as pupil—but to whom? Freud does not name Sigmund Exner or Ernst Fleischl, whom he later called his models (Freud 1925, p. 9). Neither do we see the names of Josef Breuer or Wilhelm Fliess or even Theodor Meynert, whom Freud designated the most brilliant genius he ever met (Jones 1953, p. 65; cf. Freud 1900, p. 437). Our curiosity is both quenched and refired as we catch sight of two revered names flowing from Freud's pen: Ernst Brücke and Jean-Martin Charcot.[1]

Leaving the scene, we now stand before the shelved volumes of Freud in our library. Looking first to see what Freud had to say about Brücke, we find to our surprise that Freud seldom mentioned him. Naturally Brücke's name shows up in *The Interpretation of Dreams* (1900), but then apart from a passing reference in *The Introductory Lectures* (1915–17), he does not appear again until Freud's *Autobiographical Study* of 1925, and finally in the postscript to *The Question of Lay Analysis* (1926). Not until then do we read that Brücke was unexcelled in his influence on Freud's life (Freud 1926, p. 254).

We are taken aback by the contrast between Freud's statement of Brücke's unparalleled impact and the relatively few references Freud made to him. The contrast is even stranger when we realize that in his first three years of medical school (1874–76), Freud sat in on Brücke's courses, and he worked in Brücke's laboratory from 1876 to 1882—the happiest years of his student life, he later wrote, (Freud 1900, p. 206). Freud spent eight consecutive years literally as a pupil of Brücke's. It is all the more intriguing, therefore, that Freud, the classic author of German prose, never discussed Brücke's use of language or his attitudes toward discourse.

If we look ahead, however, we need not remain in complete puzzlement, for two works published in Vienna

1. See Freud 1901, p. 325; just three years earlier Freud talked about himself as a pupil of Breuer and Charcot (Freud 1896, p. 199).

contain some pertinent remarks to enlighten us. In his autobiography, Moritz Benedikt complains that Brücke's lectures were apt to be difficult and unclear to his students (Benedikt 1906, p. 61). But even more useful to us is the biography written by Brücke's grandson, where we encounter the remarkable detail that the reserved Brücke refrained from talking, even with specialist friends, about any work in progress; only after an idea had fully matured did he feel disposed to discuss it (Brücke 1928, pp. 76–77; cf. Bernfeld 1944, p. 351). Retain this notion in mind as we return to that other master whom Freud overtly acknowledged in November 1899, Jean-Martin Charcot.

Freud was a pupil of Brücke's for eight years, but he studied with Charcot only briefly.[2] Yet that short contact, slightly more than a season in duration, had all the enduring elements of an existential encounter (cf. Ellenberger 1970, p. 436). For example, we know that Freud's stay in Paris was decisive in his turning from a neurological to a psychopathological orientation; we know too that throughout his psychoanalytic writings Freud rendered touching tribute to Charcot. Freud named his first son after Charcot during Charcot's lifetime; only after the death of Brücke, on the other hand, was his name conferred upon the third and last of Freud's sons.

The preceding reflections pique our interest as to

2. At the most, Freud saw Charcot for fifteen-and-a-half weeks, not seventeen, as claimed by Jones. Freud first met Charcot on October 20, 1885, and saw him for the last time on February 23 of the following year; on 20 December, Freud left to visit his fiancée at Wandsbek, returning nine days later (cf. Jones 1953, pp. 183, 186–87).

Freud's thoughts of Charcot's expository power, and indeed it is quite telling that Freud reveals far more about the nature of Charcot's discourse than does Charcot's own French biographer, Georges Guillain (1955). In this connection three of Freud's writings stand out: the two prefaces to his translations of Charcot and the obituary Freud wrote of him. Charcot's lectures, translated by Freud, were gathered in a pair of radically different volumes. One consisted of public lectures that had been carefully prepared before their delivery. Each of the lectures, Freud declared, "was a little work of art in construction and composition" that succeeded in delighting its audience (Freud 1893, pp. 17–18; 1956, p. 9).

But Freud was more captivated by the volume of improvised lectures, the famous *Leçons du mardi* (Tuesday lectures) that demonstrated Charcot's instructive technique in the outpatient clinic at the Salpêtrière. It did not escape Freud's observation that Charcot's *Leçons du mardi* were much more popular than the formal lectures, with all their artistry. So Freud wrote in 1893 that the publication of Charcot's improvised lectures "has . . . immeasurably widened the circle of his admirers; . . . never before has a work on neuropathology had such a success with the medical public as this" (Freud 1893, p. 18). These lectures, therefore, obviously served as an effective expository model for the spread of Freud's science. Given his artistic sensitivity and respect for effective medical teaching, we might suspect him to have scrutinized the presentational aspects of Charcot's dramatic, improvised lectures. And in fact ample evidence shows that Freud reflected seriously on the resonating appeal of Charcot's *Leçons du mardi.* Here is a composite of his analysis:

These lectures owe a peculiar charm to the fact that they are entirely, or for the most part, improvisations. The professor does not know the patient who is brought before him, or knows him only superficially. He is obliged to behave before his audience as he ordinarily does only in his medical practice, with the exception that he thinks aloud and allows his audience to take part in the course of his investigations and conjectures. (Freud 1892–94, p. 133)

One could see how, to begin with, he would stand undecided in the face of some new manifestation which was hard to interpret, one could follow the paths along which he endeavoured to arrive at an understanding of it, one could study the way in which he took stock difficulties and overcame them. (Freud 1956, p. 10)

He never appeared greater to his audience than when, by giving the most detailed account of his processes of thought and by showing the greatest frankness about his doubts and hesitations, he had thus sought to narrow the gulf between teacher and pupil. (Freud 1893, p. 18)

Interest in a lecture was often properly aroused only when the diagnosis had been made and the case had been dealt with in accordance with its peculiarities. . . . It was then that—spellbound by the narrator's artistry no less than by the observer's penetration—we listened to the little stories which showed how a medical experience led up to a new discovery; it was then that, along with our teacher, we were carried up from the consideration of a clinical picture in nervous disease to a discussion of some fundamental problem of disease in general. (Freud 1892–94, p. 135)

Before we move on, let us pause to list the qualities of "peculiar charm" proper to the *Leçons du mardi* that so attracted Freud. They include frankness and courageous thinking out loud; the democratic appeal to the audience in a communal scientific venture; the disclosure of sudden doubts, hesitations, and obstacles; a concern for tracing origins; and a consideration of the broader implications of the subject at hand. But our list would be misleading if we did not append to it an incidental yet highly significant detail. Freud's style in translating Charcot's formal lectures was strikingly different from that he used in translating the informal lectures. Whereas in translating the formal lectures Freud attempted merely to render the source text, in translating the informal lectures he interspersed through the whole his own notes of explanation and even objections. Thus, with a gesture imitative of the nature of the original text, Freud interfused his translation with a dialogic openness. Such a translation is more than rendition—it is a translation elaborated by a critical dialogue itself a mimetic response to the character of the source text. Freud explained his elaborations as "critical objections and glosses such as might occur to a member of the audience"; he also mentioned the right of a reviewer in a technical journal to criticize the text being reviewed. As if that were not enough, Freud then asked that his addenda be judged on their own account by Charcot's readers (Freud 1892–94, p. 136)—thereby augmenting the dialogic appeal of the original text still further, so that we as readers of his translation are invited into a critical discussion with both him and Charcot.

At this juncture, some readers may be silently wondering, how does all this apply to Freud's own writing? Such reserve is quite justified, and I readily acknowledge that it demands an answer adequate to its implied challenge. In reply, I turn to Freud's *New Introductory Lectures* of 1933 (*GW* 15:9/*SE* 22:9) and the later *Some Elementary Lessons in Psycho-analysis* (1940b—*GW* 17:141/*SE* 23:281). Freud contrasted so-called dogmatic with genetic exposition. By combining these two treatises with *The Question of Lay Analysis* (1926) and *An Outline of Psycho-analysis* (1940a), we can contrast Freud's two types of writing. Let us begin with the dogmatic, which is formal in expression. This subject is of the utmost importance, for the dogmatic kind of discourse has received tacit, semi-official endorsement from organized psychoanalysis—if one can judge from the restrictive interpretation of Freud's work found so frequently in psychoanalytic teaching programs and in the type of expository procedure apparently favored by some psychoanalytic editorial committees.

From a number of scattered passages we may gather the five characteristics that Freud ascribed to dogmatic discourse. First, its aim is to expound rather than "to compel belief or to arouse conviction" (Freud 1940a, p. 144; cf. 1940b, p. 281). Second, its procedure is deductive in that the writer begins by stating his or her conclusions. Third, the procedure, while having a striking and impressive effect, "makes demands upon the audience's attention" (Freud 1940b, p. 281). Fourth, the dogmatic tenets are likely to be set "in the most compressed form and the most decisive version" (Freud 1940a).[3] Last, the reader obtains

3. Strachey's translation, "in the most concise form and in the most unequivocal terms," does not accurately render the German "in gedrängtester Form und in entschiedenster Fassung"—Strachey's rendering eliminates the possibility left open by Freud that one might

the impression of "an apparently self-contained whole" and a "complete theoretical structure" (Freud 1940a, p. 281; 1926, p. 191).

Let us now turn to the second kind of writing, which Freud called the genetic or historical and which he particularly liked. Although it is difficult to circumscribe, a genetic procedure can be said to demand that the writer expose his own investigative path to the reader. Of course, an author can choose to combine a dogmatic and genetic exposition—and in fact Freud was expressly concerned with this possibility literally at both ends of his psychoanalytic career. Thus, in a letter written to Breuer on 29 June 1892, we find Freud pondering how he and Breuer should organize their *Studies on Hysteria:* "The main question, no doubt, is whether we should describe it historically and lead off with all (or two) of the best case histories, or whether, on the other hand, we should start by dogmatically stating the theories we have devised as an explanation" (Freud 1940–41, p. 147). At the other end of his life span, in *Some Elementary Lessons in Psycho-analysis*, Freud returned to the problem of organization, claiming explicitly that he would use both genetic and dogmatic methods of presentation (1940b, pp. 281–82).

Armed with these considerations, we are now prepared to enter into our subject. Freud's genetic procedure was of two types, the more public one and the more private one,

---

abandon indecision in order to adopt equivocal expression most decisively. Through oversight the editors of the *Gesammelte Werke* neglected to print the short preface to the *Outline;* the text of the preface, however, is found in the original edition published in the *Internationale Zeitschrift für Psychoanalyse 25* (1940): 8.

which we shall deal with shortly. The overt aim of public genetic discourse, according to Freud, is to convince, to persuade. The writer's means of persuasion is not just to follow his earlier investigative path but to reenact it[4] with the wary "critical reader," who is consequently embarked on an adventure of trial and error. Here is Freud's elaboration of this expository process:

> It is possible to start off from what every reader knows (or thinks he knows) and regards as self-evident, without in the first instance contradicting him. An opportunity will soon occur for drawing his attention to facts in the same field which, though they are known to him, he has so far neglected or insufficiently appreciated. Beginning from these, one can introduce further facts to him of which he has *no* knowledge and so prepare him for the necessity of going beyond his earlier judgments, of seeking new points of view and of taking new hypotheses into consideration. In this way one can get him to take a part in building up a new theory about the subject and one can deal with his objections during the actual course of the joint work.   (Freud 1940b, p. 281)

In light of this elaboration, it is significant that Freud used the public genetic procedure in his first extended survey of psychoanalysis, delivered at Clark University in 1909. That survey, known to us as the "Five Lectures on Psycho-analysis," originally bore the revealing title "The Origins and Development of Psycho-analysis."

For a more extraordinary example of Freud's public

4. Cf. Roy Schafer's germane contention: "Barbara H. Smith, a literary scholar, has defined narration as '*someone telling someone else that something happened.*' I suggest that the definition should also include telling someone else that something *is* happening or *is anticipated*" (Schafer 1981, p. 4).

genetic mode, we may refer to his *Introductory Lectures,* expounded to a Viennese audience from 1915 to 1917. While replying to imaginary objections, Freud shaped his lectures in three developmental patterns: he constantly alluded to the history of psychoanalytic discovery and the current state of knowledge; he frequently discussed the development of the analytic patient's self-awareness; and he gradually educated his audience about psychoanalytic tenets. Throughout the admirably orchestrated discussion of these three strands, Freud sought for more than just transmission of intellectual knowledge to his Viennese listeners: on no less than four occasions, he asked that they suspend their judgment in order "to let the material work on them" (auf sich wirken lassen; *GW* 11:250/Freud 1915–17, p. 243; cf. also 1915–17, pp. 12, 79, 244, 431). A splendid educator, Freud attempted to approximate[5] progress in analytic treatment in his public genetic writing; hence aiming not only to stimulate his audience into thinking and feeling but also to contend with their resistances and to facilitate their associative processes.

The unique quality of Freud's public genetic discourse might be better appreciated when contrasted with the bold plan that Francis Bacon, the reputed father of modern science, laid down for scientific writing in general. From the following excerpt we glimpse Bacon's spectacular and radical plan:

5. "Approximate," of course, is a key word. About a decade after the *Introductory Lectures,* however, in a discussion of the imaginary Impartial Person, Freud disavows any power to convince and proclaims that only the experience of analytic treatment can persuade a person of the truths of psychoanalysis (Freud 1926, pp. 198–99).

> Knowledge which is delivered to others . . . *should be insinuated* (if possible) *in the same method as it was first discovered.* And this very thing is certainly possible in the case of knowledge acquired through induction . . . it is certainly possible for someone more or less to revisit his own knowledge and simultaneously to retrace the path of both his ideas and his agreement; and in that way to transplant knowledge in another mind just as it grew in his own. . . . Aphorisms—in representing only portions and, as it were, morsels of knowledge—invite others also to add and donate something.[6]

Notice the arch-rational aim of Bacon's genetic conception: the writer aphoristically conveys his retraced ideas in the same, supposedly inductive order of their discovery and in that way invites the reader to complement the induction. But there is no such insistence on inductive order in Freud's approach: as he said to Jung, "I was not at all cut out to be an inductive researcher—I was entirely meant for intuition" (letter of 17 Dec. 1911, Freud 1974, p. 523). Equally important, when Freud addressed his audience, he was acutely aware of its irrationality, its resistances, and the multiple entanglements in the working through of his communication, and he guided his delivery accordingly.

Turning to Freud's private genetic procedure, we pass

6. Translation mine. The original text reads: "Scientia vero, quae aliis . . . traditur, *eadem Methodo* (si fieri possit) . . . *est insinuanda, qua primitus inventa est.* Atque hoc ipsum fieri sane potest in scientia per Inductionem acquisita . . . sane secundum majus et minus possit quis scientiam propriam revisere, et vestigia suae cognitionis simul et consensus remetiri; atque hoc pacto scientiam sic transplantare in animum alienum sicut crevit in suo. . . . Aphorismi, cum scientiarum portiones quasdam et quasi frusta tantum exhibeant, invitant ut alii etiam aliquid adjiciant et erogent" (Bacon 1623, 2:429, 431).

from discourse used to stimulate the audience's associations to that used to stimulate the writer's own. What I say here might seem arbitrarily abstract, but not if we consider what is ordinarily labeled exploratory writing. Actually most so-called exploratory writing is not exploratory as such—written in the past tense, it is rather a report about an earlier exploration. By contrast, Freud's private genetic style truly explores ongoing processes; rather than saying something preplanned, it resembles authentic free association, in which a patient speaks to find out what he is thinking. (Most psychoanalytic writers carefully remove this kind of thinking after their first drafts.)

Reflect on Cromwell's self-revelation, "A man never mounts so high, as when he does not know where he is going." This dictum Freud frequently cited (Sachs 1945, p. 67); moreover, he carried its venturesome spirit into his writing. Thus he asserted, "When I sit down to work, and take my pen in hand, I am always curious about what will come forth, and that drives me irresistibly to work" (Knoepfmacher 1979, p. 447). For a specific creative instance where writing helped verbalize and externalize inchoate, inner experience, we can summon up Freud's masterpiece. When he was writing *The Interpretation of Dreams* in 1898, Freud declared to Fliess, "I can compose the details only in the process of writing" (letter of 24 March 1898, Freud 1985, p. 305). Four months later, Freud explained to his friend that his book "completely follows the dictates of the unconscious, on the well-known principle of Itzig, the Sunday rider, 'Itzig, where are you going?' 'Do I know? Ask the horse.' I did not start a single paragraph knowing where I would end up" (letter of 7 July 1898, Freud 1985, p. 319).

In keeping with his preference for spontaneous writing, Freud harbored a reluctance to write on a publisher's request, since he felt that on such occasions his compositions would not be innerly driven. Still, although spontaneity remained his goal, Freud never abandoned his responsibility to his readership, even in those moments when his creative spontaneity was at its height: that is to say, he did not let his private spontaneity overwhelm the value he placed on the public intelligibility of accummulated scientific observations. A moment's reflection on this vital circumstance forces us to emend our previous separation of Freud's public and genetic styles, for in effect he variously blended the two styles as he continued to explore and expound his science. That blend had an enormous advantage: it generated and facilitated the associative and critical processes, Freud's in the act of writing, and ours in the act of reading him.

Characteristically set in a fragmentary rather than a comprehensive framework, Freud's style was flexibly suited to psychoanalysis as a growing science, to the unconscious as ultimately unknowable, and to verbal language itself, which can only approximate the full complexities of unconscious life. It follows that Freud was given to using flexible definitions. It follows too that, contrary to his English translators' reliance on a terminology drawn preeminently from dead classical languages, Freud preferred to use vital, everyday terms from his own living German language. He considered these words appropriate not only because "concrete terms, in consequence of the history of their development, are richer in associations than conceptual ones" (Freud 1900, p. 340) but also because of the resonance that continues to accrue from their currency in both the psychology and the psychopathology of everyday life.

The temporal aspects of Freud's genetic discourse bear utmost significance, and this in spite of the fact that one shifts tenses much more often in German than, say, in English. Readers of the English *Standard Edition* of Freud's work cannot appreciate, for example, that in the Rat Man case Freud renders five different temporal scenes in the present tense: the Rat Man's childhood, his psychoanalytic treatment, Freud's process notes, his subsequent revision of them for the published case history, and finally, Freud's enlisting of readers as clinical co-observers (Mahony 1986, pp. 184–87). This five-track stereophonic prose is rendered simply in the past tense in Strachey's translation.[7] Let me emphasize that the issue at hand is not a matter of superficial aesthetics; it concerns the primary process of Freud's prose, its psychodynamics, and its accumulative impact on the reader. Yet as rich as is Freud's original German text, it becomes even richer if we momentarily shift to a higher theoretical level.

Elliott Jaques' *The Form of Time* (1982) comes to our assistance here. Jaques elucidates how we oscillate between the cognitive conception of a continuous field and

7. According to Ornston (1982), Freud always describes his important concepts in several different ways, but Strachey dropped this descriptive flexibility, aiming for more consistency in his translation. The subjunctive Freud often used to convey uncertainty about unconscious processes Strachey tended to change into the indicative mode of factual statement. For other pertinent studies by Ornston, see the bibliography.

that of a field of discrete objects. From the unconscious and preconscious processes comes the experience of time as flux, as the interaction of memory with the perceptual present and the future of expectation and desire. In focused conscious awareness, on the other hand, one perceives an atomistic world and temporal discontinuity—from which arise discrete ideas of past and future time.[8] In contrast with the nonverbal primal flow of the unconscious and the unformed and unconnected preconscious awareness, conscious perception is focused and verbal. The separateness of words goes against the continuity of preconscious and unconscious experience: the flux of time, as Hegel says, is killed by words. It stands to reason, therefore, that continuity is best mirrored not by scientifically rigorous language but by poetic language in all its evocativeness (see Jaques 1982, esp. pp. 52, 57–60, 65).

I suggest that Freud's "five-track stereophonic" style, which collapses various times into the present, is evidence of the impact of unconscious processes upon his imagination. As a counterpoint stands Freud's exceptional concern with time as a series of discrete units. Continually anticipating what is to come and looking back to what has already been said, Freud orients the reader to the sequence of historical and psychic realities and their textual exposition (Mahony 1987). Accordingly, in their presentation of time as both in flux and discrete, Freud's temporally concerned texts give readers a well-rounded conscious and unconscious experience. But temporal permeation is not the only

8. In this connection, see Gilbert Rose's comments on the effect of primary process on spatial and temporal experience (Rose 1980, esp. pp. 10–12).

element that is masterfully balanced between conscious and unconscious expression in Freud's open-ended textuality. Brilliant critical analysis also shakes hands with evocative language, whose frequency and intensity may serve as a measure of Freud's impulsively inspired exploratory discourse. In a similar vein, Freud includes rather than flushes out tangential remarks; he is even likely to highlight their tangentiality. Or after setting up a certain number of categories for discussion of a particular subject, Freud may add categories later—without revising his earlier list. By such means Freud retains for the reader the associative freshness of his text.

Traditional psychoanalytic teaching has duly focused on the narrow scene of discourse between analyst and patient, sometimes critically slighting the larger scene of discourse among analysts, including Freud, writing and speaking to one another. Perhaps that imbalance has been influenced by Strachey, who included throughout the *Standard Edition* a number of lists superficially categorizing Freud's writing according to subject matter. I have attempted to go underneath those lists and propose a dynamically grounded taxonomy of Freud's works. Such a dynamic taxonomy has far-reaching implications for how we read Freud, teach him, write about him, and listen to our patients. (No definitive break exists between any of these activities.)

Recall our leaving Freud bent over for a period at his writing desk. If we now require of ourselves an even greater imaginary displacement, we might accompany Freud in his composition of numerous writings over four decades. In this venture we should be mindful that punctuation, like language, has manifest as well as latent aspects, and we should accordingly take into account that each of Freud's works ends not with a period but with an ellipsis. Such suspensive punctuation characterizes the essentially fragmentary nature of all psychoanalytic ventures, including this, in its analyses authentically interminable . . .

In the next chapter we rejoin Freud in his office, but this time he himself will take us to another place, a mountain lookout in southern Austria, and there we will see with him, beyond him, the promise of his lofty conceptions and touching formulations. More important, a particular text—the case of Katharina—will enable us better to appreciate, in the concrete, features of Freud's discourse which we have examined up to now only in general outlines.

2

The Dawn of Psychoanalysis:
Katharina's Case History

Freud, from the very beginning of his career, was explicitly concerned with the strategic combining of genetic and dogmatic style. In this regard the final plan drawn up for *Studies on Hysteria* is worth our scrutiny. This work of collaboration between Freud and Josef Breuer has four sections. The first, third, and fourth of these are written dogmatically, yet arranged in chronological order. The first section was originally published by the collaborators in January 1893; the third and fourth sections were written by Breuer and Freud respectively for the completed book, published in 1895. The following tableau indicates the chronological arrangement of the five case histories of the second section; in all, they span some thirteen years, beginning with Anna O. (the only case of the five treated by Breuer):

1. Anna O.—December 1880 to June 1882
2. Frau Emmy—seven or eight weeks between 1889 and 1890
3. Lucy—December 1892 to February 1893

4. Katharina—August 1893
5. Elisabeth—fall 1892 to summer 1893

Each of Freud's case histories has two parts, a historical account of the illness and treatment and a discussion, which proceeds mostly in a dogmatic fashion. Hence the larger structure of *Studies on Hysteria* is more or less replicated in the case histories that constitute it. Among these, the case of Katharina has the most stylistic merit.

There is nothing else in the whole Freudian corpus quite like the case of Katharina, the shortest of all his case histories. As we shall see, the many textual riches of the case lay long exposed on or about the surface, waiting patiently to be gathered; in recomposing them we shall be in a position to nuance our previous categorizations of Freud's discourse. But first of all, let us familiarize ourselves with the case through a pair of updated historical and clinical recontextualizations.

Freud tells us that it was during the summer of 189– that he hiked up one of the higher mountains in the Austrian Alps. After pausing for refreshment in a refuge hut on the mountainside, he continued his climb to a lookout and fell into deep contemplation of the charming scenery. In the midst of his musing he was interrupted by the sulky-looking Katharina, the daughter of the hut's landlady, who had noticed the medical title attached to Freud's signature in the visitors' book. A case of "bad nerves" that had proved unresponsive to a medical consultation led the eighteen-year-old girl to bespeak her troubles to Freud. Her symptoms, which included breathlessness and fear of a hallucinated, dreadful, yet unidentifiable face, had begun two years earlier. One Friday, two climbers had stopped by the hut and asked for something to eat. Their mother was away, so Katharina and her younger brother, Alois, went in search of Franziska, the cook, and then looked for their father. As a last resort, the children tried their father's bedroom door. Finding it locked, they went around to the corridor window. Alois fearfully shrank away, but Katharina looked through the window and saw her father lying atop Franziska. Katharina turned aside, searching for her breath; her head was hammering and everything went blank. By Monday her symptoms had worsened and she had to spend several days in bed. Finally she told her mother of her discovery; family arguments followed, and the mother moved with the children to another inn on a neighboring mountain, leaving her husband behind with Franziska, who eventually became pregnant.

Continuing her narration to Freud, Katharina brought in still earlier experiences. At fourteen, she had accompanied her father on an expedition into the valley. They spent the night in an inn, where her father came into her bed and pressed his body against hers. She told Freud additional stories of defending herself against the sexual advances of her drunken father, and she described several more occasions on which she had observed something taking place between him and Franziska. Then, suddenly, she stopped speaking, seeming relieved, even transformed. When Freud asked her what part of her father's body she had felt during the night at the inn, she smiled in embarrassment, as if she had been found out. She then said that the hallucinated face in her recurrent attacks was her father's, and that it stemmed from her parents' quarrels over

Franziska, in which her enraged father accused Katharina of causing the whole conflict. Later, when her parents were discussing separation, Katharina reported to her mother her father's attempts at incestuous seduction.

Recent research has helped fill in some of the details of Katharina's background. Her paternal grandfather, Johann Kronich, was born in Vienna around 1818. In 1849, with a woman who had previously given birth to children of unknown paternity, he fathered an illegitimate son named Julius. Johann Kronich married the woman two years later, and they subsequently had another child, Hermine, who herself went on to have two illegitimate children.

In May 1873 the twenty-three-year-old Julius Kronich married Gertrude, his elder by five years, and together they had five children: Julius (1873), Aurelia Katharina (January 1875), Camillo (1876), Bruno (1877), and Olga (1878). Around 1885, prompted by his alarming tuberculoid condition, the elder Julius Kronich moved with his family from Vienna to run the mountain lodge Baumgartnerhaus on the Schneeberg, fifty miles south of Vienna. The sizable lodge, which had about sixty beds, was at an altitude of nearly forty-nine hundred feet, some two thousand feet from the mountain's summit. From the valley one could reach the lodge by pack animal or several hours of strenuous hiking; similarly, going down to the valley to fetch supplies took the better part of a day and sometimes necessitated an overnight stay. These traveling conditions, plus the fact that the lodge was often snowed in during the winter, made it necessary that the mountaineers' school-age children be housed in a village down the mountain; they returned to the lodge on weekends and summer holidays.

Katharina was not a simple, innocent country girl, as is suggested in Freud's case history; in fact, her background helps to highlight her hysterical dissociation, of both knowing and not-knowing. First, she had ample opportunity to observe farm animals in heat and copulation. Second, she had lived for some ten years in Vienna. She could play at least one musical instrument and was a member of a choir; she and one of her brothers were known for their talents and were invited to sing and yodel at various local activities and apparently even in Vienna. Pertinently, however, in the end Katharina did not pursue a singing career, which she considered an immoral profession.

In contrast to his proper daughter, Julius Kronich, according to family legend, was reckless, a heavy drinker, and a womanizer. He probably carried on an affair with his wife's niece Barbara, sixteen years his junior, whose father had supposedly been a village priest. Employed as a cook in the nearby village of Reichenau, Barbara could have conveniently been invited to lend an occasional helping hand in the Baumgartnerhaus; presumably she was the cook, cousin Franziska, in Freud's case history.

Early in 1893, Frau Kronich separated[1] from her husband and moved with her children to the neighboring massif, Raxalpe, to take charge of the Erzherzog Otto Schutzhaus (Archduke Otto refuge hut), newly built by the Austrian Alpine Society. A recently constructed road (Thörlweg) meant the hut was but a three hours' walk from

---

1. *Scheidung* usually means "divorce" (Strachey's translation) but is also used for "separation." There is no surviving document to indicate that Julius was divorced; this, plus the conservative attitude of the church at the time, suggests that the couple was merely separated.

Reichenau, an international resort whose distinguished guests were entertained by concerts, theatrical performances, and other festivities; Freud passed some summers there with his family in the 1890s, and in the decisive year of 1893, he was among four thousand guests who visited the new and long-awaited lodge on the Raxalpe. Yet our young heroine could have had no inkling that Freud had already established himself as a foremost neurologist and that he would soon enshrine her story in the first classic of a new science.

Momentarily looking beyond the memorable meeting between Freud and Katharina, I note here several details of her later life. Apparently shortness of breath did not bother her again; she never consulted another nerve specialist. She married in September 1895 and had six children and perhaps the same number of miscarriages. It is hardly accidental that Julius, the name she gave to her firstborn son, was the name not only of Katharina's father but also of her favorite brother and her husband. Nor did Freud drop out of the picture: during a vacation in the early 1900s, he was called on to treat the fever and abdominal pains of one of Katharina's daughters, and around 1920 he received one of her sons in consultation in Vienna.[2]

We now pass on to the comparative diagnosis of Katharina, a promising subject which brings us nearer to an

2. For supplementary biographical information, I am indebted to Swales (1988) and Fichtner and Hirschmüller (1985); the former essay is especially rich in historical matters. I have merely the following to add. While Freud stayed on working in Vienna, his family left for Reichenau on 1 June 1893. Before giving up his office work to-

understanding of the intricate prose used in constructing her case history. Freud explicitly set forth his clinical conception of Katharina's pathology as follows. Katharina's anxiety arose from combined anxiety and hysterical neurosis, the former creating the symptoms and the latter repeating and operating with them (Freud 1893–95, p. 260). The hysteria itself was acquired and as such merely suggested a widespread proclivity to acquire hysteria; specifically, Katharina did not manifest a neuropathic condition prior to the illness and traceable to a "hereditary taint" or the accumulation of her "individual psychical abnormalities" (pp. 122, 133). Freud's position here is at a certain distance from his previous endorsement of Charcot's idea, presented in the *Leçons du mardi*, that heredity is the "true cause" of hysteria (Freud 1892–94, p. 139).[3] Not until 1897 did Freud, in his postulation of the Oedipus complex, clearly grasp hysteria as an infantile neurosis with a sexual etiology, yet in the early 1890s he already was claiming that the so-called actual neuroses—anxiety neurosis and neurasthenia—were caused by absence or insufficiency of sexual activity. Central to this formulation was

---

ward the end of July to join his family (Freud 1985, pp. 49, 52), he visited them in Reichenau in June and July; during July Freud met Lucy, Katharina's predecessor in the *Studies on Hysteria* (Freud 1893–95, pp. 106, 121). It is quite possible that Lucy took the children in her care to attend one of Katharina's singing and yodeling exhibitions during that summer.

3. Although the exact dating of Freud's translation of the *Leçons du mardi* is problematic, we do know that even six months before he met Katharina, Freud was entertaining the notion of anxiety neurosis as acquired.

Freud's toxological theory of anxiety as the transformation of dammed-up libido. According to Freud, that transformed libido marked the first encounter of virgins such as Katharina (pp. 127, 134) with sexuality.[4]

Relevant to our impending textual analysis is the fact that, specifically as regards interpsychic dynamics, contemporary clinical scrutiny of Katharina's case history has gone beyond Freud's early position. First, Freud's drive-discharge and toxological theory has given way to an understanding of hysteria in terms of meanings, motives, and identifications. Consequently, a principal feature in Katharina's psychodynamics is victimization, the internalization of which is not simply a one-to-one interaction but rather involves multiple objects relating complexly at various stages of development. Also bearing on Katharina's psychic formation were her simultaneous or alternating double identifications in possible earlier experiences of primal scenes, her mother's and father's mutual victimization of each other, the mother's possible collusion in the family incest, and Katharina's identification with Franziska and possibly with the oedipal mother as the father's sexual victims (indicated in her hysterical symptoms of breathlessness).[5] What is more, the phobic, projective quality of Ka-

4. Taking up his earlier ideas about virginal anxiety (Freud 1985 pp. 49, 80–81), Freud wrote in an essay published in January 1895 that women like Katharina, upon their initial encounter with sexuality, break out in a combined anxiety and hysterical neurosis (1895, pp. 98–98). But in a paper finished in February of the next year, Freud corrects his former idea and says that the adult neurosis of virgins relies on a sexually passive experience in their childhood (1896b, p. 166 and n.).

5. Freud outlined three stages in Katharina's reaction to the

tharina's anxiety symptoms entailed an externalization of her fantasies; thus she saw herself as victimized and hallucinated a persecuting face. At the same time, an unresolved ambivalence colored her identification in the hallucination. In turn, Katharina's guilt over her parents' separation was perhaps fueled by a latent wish to victimize them, both because of penis envy and because of her subordination as a woman; thus filial revenge had as one of its consequences

---

traumatizing love scene between her father and Franziska:

1. Katharina at once [*sofort*] made connections with her own previous sexual experiences; yet while understanding them, she concomitantly began "to fend them off." The anxiety marking this struggle was a consequence of the horror that the virginal Katharina experienced on first confronting sexuality. Involved in that anxiety was a complex of physical sensations: shortness of breath, blankness, pressure on her eyelids, and a hammering and buzzing in her head.

2. A three-day period of incubation followed, in which continuing anxiety created a hypnoid state whose products were then [*dann*] cut off from associative connection with ego-consciousness; more precisely, Katharina began to forget the details of what she saw through the window.

3. After the incubation, she was bedridden for three days and underwent the conversion symptoms of vomiting. According to the pictographic script of hysterical symptomatology, the vomiting was a substitute for physical and moral disgust (see also Freud 1896a, pp. 193–94; Nunberg and Federn 1967–75, 4:131–32); through the vomiting, the hysteria was also considerably abreacted.

The importance of the word *sofort* in stage 1 has eluded commentators—by using it, Freud subtly indicated his theoretical difference with Breuer. According to Breuer, in hypnoid hysteria an idea becomes pathological when it emerges during a special psychic state; therefore it remains outside the ego from the very beginning. For Freud, on the other hand, such psychical splitting is itself activated by defense (Freud 1893–95, pp. 285–86; cf. the erroneous conclusion of Glenn 1980, p. 38).

the elimination of the mother from the marriage bed (Meissner 1979). The foregoing theses, of course, are considerably supported by the new information on the impulsiveness of Julius Kronich and chaotic structure of his family.

Again and again, modern critics have emphasized oedipal factors in Katharina's case—the mutual desire between her and her father; her repressed murderous jealousy of her rival, Franziska, and her punishment by betrayal of both Franziska and the unfaithful father; the daughterly recourse to revenge in order to protect herself against future incestuous temptations; and, finally, repressed guilt toward the mother, partly manifested by vomiting, which also signified Katharina's self-disgust over not being able to tell her mother of the scene (Glenn 1980; Anzieu 1975; Argelander 1976). In sum, her ability to relate well to Freud and to split her ego for the purpose of remembering without suffering another attack, as an acting-out hysteric might have, indicates that Katharina may be seen as a classic hysteric with sufficient preoedipal personality development. The very scene of Katharina's discovery of her father with Franziska constitutes the unconscious core of the interview with Freud. Accordingly, Katharina's mountaintop consultation is characterized by primal-scene material and by fears of being discovered and betrayed, in which she identifies herself with Franziska, whom she refers to as *Mädel*, the colloquial expression for young girl, maid, and sweetheart (see also Argelander 1976, 1978).

The preceding comments are all very well and good as applied to Katharina, but what was the impact of such dy-

namics on Freud, the consultant and writer? The answer is
manifold. Note first that although Katharina was the target
of paternal anger because of her reporting the tryst and the
incest, she felt different with Freud—"you can say *anything* to a doctor."[6] Counterbalancing this, Freud employs
a suggestive series of references to Katharina. He guesses
that the person interrupting him is not just a simple *Magd*
(servant—in its more restricted, literary use, *Magd* means
"maiden" or "virgin," hence anticipating some of the story's dynamics). In postulating the sexual innocence of the
fourteen-year-old Katharina, he alludes to her as a "child"
in her "pre-sexual period"; immediately afterward, however, he doubts her sexual innocence at that time and
groups her with "adolescents" and "virginal persons" (pp.
194–95/133–34).[7]

Alerted by these epithets, we are now prepared to see
that Freud's narrative contains a series of skillfully wrought
sexual allusions:

1. Freud points to the virgin's anxiety, which occurs
when the sexual world "opens up" (*sich auftut*) before her,
a sexual suggestiveness which is lost in Strachey's passive
version: "is faced with." In his "Discussion," Freud repeats
the suggestion, using *sich erschlossen hat* as a synonym for
sich auftut: memories may have a deferred traumatic effect
"when the understanding of sexual life has opened itself to

6. "Anything" is not italicized in *GW*, nor are five of the six
other instances of italicized words in the English translation of the
case history. Here, as elsewhere, Strachey's italics often involve his
own free associations to Freud's text.

7. Two sets of page numbers separated by a slash refer to
Gesammelte Werke (vol. 1) and *Standard Edition* (vol. 2) respectively.

the virgin or woman" [*wenn sich der Jungfrau oder Frau das Verständnis des sexuellen Lebens erschlossen hat*].[8] Once more, Freud's suggestiveness is effaced by Strachey, who turns the clause around, this time making the woman the active subject rather than the passive object: "when the girl or married woman has acquired an understanding of sexual life."

2. The statement about Katharina's discovery of her father and Franziska, which translates as "they both of them had their clothes on" (*die waren ja beide angezogen [in Kleidern].*), has a more striking effect in German. *Angezogen* in German most often means "dressed," but it can also mean "pulled" or "attracted." By adding *in Kleidern* (in clothes) in parentheses, Freud humorously intends us to juggle the meanings of dressed, pulled, and attracted. Finally, the German word for "parentheses" is *runde Klammern; Klammern* itself signifies objects that fasten or tighten—the clothes themselves are such fasteners or tighteners, ironically bound within typographical fasteners!

3. In response to the query as to what part of her father's body she had felt in bed, Katharina reacted (according to Strachey's translation) "like someone who is obliged to admit that a fundamental position has been reached where there is not much more to be said." But the phrase "fundamental position" does not adequately render the simpler German *Grund der Dinge* (literally, "ground of the thing"), which plainly refers to the father's penis. Further-

8. Cf. Freud's comment on Dora's first dream: "The question whether a woman is 'open' or 'shut' can naturally not be a matter of indifference" (1905, p. 67 n).

more, the use of *Grund* (ground) recapitulates the thematic verticality in a story of a mountaintop conversation about down-to-earth things.

4. Freud found it easier to talk with the candid Katharina than with the prudish ladies of his city practice, who held that whatever is natural (*naturalia*) is obscene (*turpia*). In other texts, Freud sometimes used Latin because of his own reserve; here, however, he used Latin ironically, to compare the evasive talk of his Viennese ladies with Katharina's directness. Once more we can enhance our appreciation by comparatively referring to Strachey's translation, for not only is the irony of Freud's Latin phrase (*naturalia turpia*) lost in Strachey's English rendering but even the erotic force of *turpia* (obscene) is toned down: Strachey has Freud saying that the city ladies "regard whatever is natural as shameful."

Proceeding further into Freud's text, we notice that Katharina's sexually saturated, traumatic history provokes more than just an eroticized lexicality in Freud's narrative. It provoked a lexicality whose erotic notes are enmeshed rather than simply juxtaposed—indicative of Freud's very deep sexual reaction to Katharina. His sexual involvement is displayed in references to copulation and birth (found chiefly in vertical images), scopophilia, and the play of deictics, which I shall now explain.

Let us start by scrutinizing the German roots *fall* and *stand*, which verily drench Freud's case history exceeding their frequent occurrence in ordinary contexts. A short sampling will perhaps be suggestive, especially in combination with other vertical references. Having reached the *top* of a mountain outlook in the *Hohe* (high) Tauern,

Freud sat deep (ver*sunk*en) in contemplation. He then *fell* into a conversation with Katharina (Die *Unterredung, die jetzt zwischen uns* vor*fiel*), who talked about her anxiety attack (Angstan*fall*)[9] and her condition (Zu*stand*) of dyspnea and of feeling so giddy that she could almost fall over (*fall*'um). Humorously reflecting that he could not hypnotize her at such high altitudes (*Höhen*), Freud thought about the sexual anxiety that befalls (be*fällt*) the virginal mind. Freud spoke recurrently of Katharina's attacks (An*fälle*) and referred to her hypnoid condition (Zu*stand*) whose products *stand* outside[10] associative connection with ego-consciousness. Freud writes that he "told her to go on and tell me whatever occurred [*einfiele*, from ein*fallen*] to her, in the confident expectation that she would think [ein*fallen*] of precisely what I needed to explain the case [*Falles*]" (189/129). Katharina compliantly begins her story, elaborating on how strange [auf*fällig*] it was that her father's room was locked, and later drops [lässt *fall*en] the thread to recount other sexual activities of her father, about which she had no suspicion at the time: "I only just noticed [auf*gefall*en] it and thought no more about it." Included in

9. *Paradise Lost* is a literary work known for its masterly orchestration of vertical references. Pertinently, Milton also works the very activity of under*stand*ing into his architectonics of verticality. In the Katharina case, the question of understanding (Ver*ständ*nis, Ver*stehen*) naturally comes up several times; but the very understanding of that word within a network of unconscious derivatives is another matter. Likewise, in thinking about how Freud turned off the main road (*Hauptstrasse*), one should bear in mind that "main" does not render another meaning of *Haupt*—head—which fits in both with the neurosis and the verticality of mountain climbing.

10. Cf. Strachey's translation: "were cut off" (p. 128).

her attacks of vomiting[11] was the memory, as Freud worded it, of her father's "nighttime assault" [Über*fall*][12] on her in the valley inn.

Although some of the vertical imagery was unavoidable, its exceptional frequency ultimately stems from an overdetermined synergy between Freud and Katharina. The same unconscious material left its mark not only on the lexical items reproducing the exchange but also on those used to comment on the exchange. We know from Freud's letter to Wilhelm Fliess in August 1893 that he and Martha were abstaining from sexual activity; furthermore, he had been climbing around the Raxalpe for two days. Pertinent too is a card that Freud sent to Oskar Pfister in June 1928, which bore the following retrospection and textual reference: "A few days ago I myself was up on the Rax (6,000 feet), which a few decades ago I used to climb three times a week" (Freud 1963, p. 124). Whatever purposes the habitual climbing served for Freud, it was certainly in part an attempt to divert himself during his enforced abstinence. We might notice too that three times in print Freud himself underscored that the German *steigen* means both "to climb" and "to copulate" (Freud 1900, p. 355; 1910b, p. 143;

11. Katharina's reactive vomiting was also her symbolic way of bodily expelling her father and the cook, Franziska, along with her undesirable food (see also n. 5, above; I am grateful to Stef Jones and Danny Swarzman for the latter observation). Strachey translates *Erbrechen* first by "vomiting" (189/129) and then by "getting sick" (193/132); the latter unfortunately obscures the notion of symbolic expulsion.

12. Strachey's translation, "the attempt on her at night," tones down the violence of *nächtlichen Überfall*, which is often used in the military sense of a nighttime raid.

1915–17, p. 164), a coincidence bearing significantly on the explicit and implicit erotic derivatives in Katharina's case history.

Interacting with the overdetermined meaning of *steigen*, Katharina's fantasy life had a subtle impact on the lexicality of the case history, observable through her sensations of falling and their significance as fantasies of giving birth. Freud later made use of the double meaning of *niederkommen* ("to fall down" and "to give birth") in interpreting little Hans's concern that "the horses'll fall down" (Freud 1909, p. 96); there was also the case of the homosexual woman who attempted suicide by "falling down" before a train, thus symbolically fulfilling a wish to have a child by her father, who had spurned her (Freud 1920, p. 120 n). Intimately associated with Katharina's meaningful falling sensations are her feelings of disgust and of being cheated, which also form part of the pictographic script of her hysterical symptomatology. The word Katharina employs to indicate her "dizzy" sensations before almost falling is *schwindlich*, whose verbal form, *schwindeln*, means both "to feel dizzy" and "to cheat" (see also Nunberg and Federn 1967, pp. 135–36). Desiring a child from her father, Katharina is "disgusted" with herself and also with him, for he is unfaithful, "cheating" on her. Expressive of her fear that her father might grab or catch her (*packt*, pp. 186/126, 193/132), one of her symptoms reads: "But sometimes it catches (*packt's*) me so that I think I shall suffocate" (185/125). Her anxiety stems in part from the satisfaction of her sexual curiosity and from her having "caught" (*erwischt*, 187/127) her disloyal father in bed with the cook.

Katharina's pregnancy fantasies and a related numerical symbolism may have had a postponed impact in her life. It was on a Friday that she caught her adulterous father; she worked until Monday, then went to bed for three days—all in all, a period of six days, of which three were spent in bed. Here it is important that Katharina had three younger siblings and that she went on to have six children and perhaps an equal number of miscarriages. Another indication of her oedipal fantasies as well as her mortal guilt about them is her particular choice of interjection—*Jesses*—which, incidentally, Strachey translates as "Heavens" (187/127) and "Goodness" (191/130). We can begin to appreciate the extraordinary import of *Jesses* when we realize that not only is it a corruption of *Jesus* but also it phonetically resembles *Julius*, the name of Katharina's father, favorite brother, and, later, her husband and firstborn son.

At one point in Freud's text, his self-reflective expository language engages upon a full sexual exploration but stops short of violent imposition. Thus, after interpreting Katharina's disgust as directed only against her father, Freud resorts to flattery in order to encourage her to recognize and name the sensation of her father's penis against her: "'Tell me just one thing more,'" Freud reports he said. "'You're a grown-up girl now and know all sorts of things. . . . Tell me just one thing. What part of his body was it that you felt that night?' But she gave no more definite answer. She smiled in an embarrassed way" (pp. 131–32). Unlike Katharina's sexually unscrupulous father, Freud halts his exploration, saying, "But I could not penetrate [*dringen*] further." The phrase, equally suggestive in

English and German, testifies to the sexualization of Freud's discourse as an expressive and communicative medium.

A short step brings us to the textually marked scopophilia, whose active and passive aspects are to some degree summed up in *Gesicht,* meaning both "face" and "sight" or "vision." We recall that Katharina figured frequently in singing exhibitions and that for moral reasons she forsook a career in singing. Significantly, after having seen in the visitors' book that Freud was a doctor, she proceeded to consult him at the outlook. There Freud observed that she had an "unhappy look" and was rather "sulky-looking"; she went on to describe her attacks. Relevantly, they affected her sight (she felt dizzy and felt something pressing on her eyes). Despite her denial that she and her younger brother suspected their father, the boy obviously did, for he was too frightened to look in the corridor window. Katharina looked but claimed she could not see anything because of the dark. Yet she did observe that the bedded couple was clothed and that Franziska's face did not have the awful look of the hallucinated face that afterward pursued her and made her frightened of being caught "unawares" (*unversehens,* literally, in an unexpected or unforeseen way). Freud's self-involvement or even self-projection in Katharina's narrative is evident when he asks her (she is now sitting beside him), "When you have an attack, do you think of something? and always the same thing? or do you see something *in front of you?*" (my italics). A scopophilic theme runs through the whole case history (lost in Strachey's translation), linking Freud, Katharina, and the reader and establishing a connection between the last sentence of the narration ("I have not seen her again") and the first sentence of the discussion: "I cannot, on the other hand, object if someone wants to look [*erblicken*] on this patient's history not so much as an analyzed case of hysteria as one solved by correctly guessing [*Erraten*]"[13] (193– 94/133; my translation).[13]

Freud's use of deictics deserves special examination, but before we venture further, a series of helpful distinctions need to be made. In the systematics of Charles Sanders Peirce, the founder of modern semiotics, a sign is one of three types: an icon, based on a factual similarity (such as the metaphor, "a camel is the ship of the desert"); an index, based on factual contiguity (e.g., "where there is smoke

13. Several additional examples of Freud's suggestiveness might be mentioned. The initial scene of climbing a mountain "laid off to the side" (*abseits gelegenen*) is echoed in Katharina's scene (*Szene*), in which an association is effected with a group of elements previous "situated off to the side" (*abseits befindlichen*). Merging therapeutic concerns with setting, Freud utters surprise that neuroses can "flourish" at such high altitudes and voices his reluctance to "transplant" hypnosis there. Perhaps these horticultural images are further suggested by the name of Katharina's first refuge hut, Baumgartnerhaus (lit., tree-gardener house). Also noticeable is Freud's imagistic extension of the story's framework of travel to the clinical context: "Perhaps a quick way was then offering itself to penetrate to the heart of the matter. . . . Then the way seemed suddenly blocked [*verlegen*]. Perhaps something can be found in the rest of her story" (translation partially mine). Gradually Freud reaches a point in his questioning at which Katharina became "embarrassed" [*verlegen*]. In his final addendum to the case history, appended thirty years later, Freud, as if by association to the story, used another meaning of *verlegen*: upon disclosing that Katharina was the daughter rather than the niece of the inn's landlady, Freud pleaded that the original distortion was less unimportant to our understanding than a shift [*Verlegung*] of the scene from one mountain to another would have been.

there is fire"); or a symbol (the learned, imputed contiguity between the constituents of a word, such as the signifier and the signified).[14] In terms of this classification, certain symbols, called deictics (from the Greek *deiktikos*, pointing), are set apart from others by their indexical character. Deictics, or shifters, are orientational features in language, dealing with the time and place of utterances. As such, verb tenses, personal pronouns (*I, you, they*), some verbs (*come, go*), and certain adverbs of place and time (here, there, now, then) constitute the spatiotemporal orientation of an utterance; demonstrative pronouns (*this, that, these, those*) qualify as deictics in that they indicate varying proximity to the speaker.

Ordinary utterance is egocentric in that, as one assumes the speaker's role in a conversation, the center of the deictic system shifts (*I* refers to the speaker, *you* to the listener). It is evident that whereas the hearer and speaker are present in the situation of an utterance, the third person (*he, she, it, they*) may or may not be. But it is less evident within this frame of reference that the plural of *I* is not simply *we*, for *we* means the speaker and one or more persons who may or may not be among the hearers. The plural of *I* is either inclusive *we* (which includes the addressee) or exclusive *we* (which does not include the addressee) (Lyons 1968). Freud's *we* tends to be inclusive. Also, like many Germans, he is given to employ spatial deictics: the recurrence of the verbal prefixes *hin* (thither, away from the speaker) and *her* (hither, toward the speaker) is unmatched in English.

14. This last pair of terms, of course, is Sausurrean.

The important linguistic notion of deixis has been woefully neglected in Anglo-American psychoanalytic literature. But the contemporary interpretive debate over transference versus reconstruction can be partially reformulated into the deictic opposition between the here-and-now and the there-and-then. In the case at hand, it is precisely through deictics that we have a privileged, verbal way of tracing some subtle feelings of Freud both as therapist and as writer (his empathy, his distance, and his overdetermined rapprochement).

Let us now put ourselves in the company of Freud during his vacation of August 1893, when he met Katharina. Around the time of their mountaintop encounter, Freud's intrapersonal and interpersonal worlds were in various ways spatially beset with considerations of remoteness, closeness, and pursuit. Such is what we read in the letter Freud addressed to Fliess from Reichenau on 20 August 1893:

> I spent the 18th and 19th on a complicated tour around and on Mount Rax with my friend Rie, and yesterday sat in a cheerful mood in the new hut on the mountain when someone entered the room, completely flushed from the heat of day, whom initially I stared at as an apparition and then had to recognize as my wife. Martha has always maintained that climbing was impossible for her and that she did not enjoy staying on the mountain. *But now she had followed me*, had borne up well under the strain, and was enchanted by the view and the place. She expressed the wish to spend several days *with me* up *here*, where the accommodations are excellent, and I felt obliged to afford her this pleasure—which is possible, so to speak, *without feeling*

remote from home, because from up here one can stay in touch with Reichenau by telephone and easily get down in two and a half hours. She had been looking forward to the trip to Csorba very much. The events at home had shown her how difficult it is to make arrangements for *leaving* the children, and for the past six years, since *child followed child,* there has been little room for change and relaxation in her life. I do not believe I can deny her this wish. You can imagine what is behind it: gratitude, a feeling of coming back to life again of the woman who for the time being does not have to expect a child for a year, because *we are now living in abstinence.* . . . Now, this plan does not at all agree with my intention to visit you in Csorba. . . . Although she never interferes with a pleasure of mine, and least of all would want to interfere with *getting together with you,* she nevertheless made the point that I only needed to give up Csorba, and not you, since ten days later I can *have you so much nearer* in Brühl [in the outskirts of Vienna]. . . . My head has not yet gotten rid of the obsession with the pursuit of medical ideas and that continuation for a while of the present way of life would be very good for it. . . . For the rest, the etiology of the neuroses *pursues me everywhere,* as the Marlborough song follows the traveling Englishman. Recently I was consulted by the daughter of the innkeeper on the Rax; it was a nice case for me. (Freud 1985, pp. 54–55; italics mine)

This interesting letter challenges some of our previous assumptions and leaves open the possibility that it was during Freud's stay at the inn that Katharina first saw him. Be that as it may, the opening of Freud's case history continues in the temporal, spatial, and personal vein of his letter to Fliess. Freud did not completely succeed in escaping from the "pursuit of medical ideas" and losing himself in nature, for Katharina wrenched him back into the concerns of therapy. In that sense Freud had attempted in vain atop Mount Rax to leave his professional commitments behind, in time (summer vacation) and in space (he was truly a considerable distance from his office horizontally as well as vertically). The particular word he chose for his relaxing excursion (*Ausflug*, lit., flying out) is quite to the point. The whole scene deserves our closer attention.

In the course of his excursion, Freud turned aside from the main road (*von der Hauptstrasse abwich*) to climb a mountain that itself was situated apart (*einen abseits gelegenen Berg*), and he finally reached it "after a strenuous, rambling hike" (*nach anstrengender Wanderung*).[15] The deviations and detours in Freud's walking tour lead to his meditative displacement, his disorienting interruption by the deictically reserved Katharina, and his self-recovery in space and time:

> I then sat, sunk deep in the contemplation of an enrapturing [*entzückenden*][16] distant sight—I was so unmindful of myself there[17] that when I heard the question,[18] "Is the gentleman a doctor?"[19] at first I did not

15. Strachey's translation of *Wanderung* by "climb" eliminates its sense of wandering or displacement.

16. Strachey's "charming" does not render the disorienting force of Freud's experience.

17. "There" is not translated by Strachey.

18. Strachey unnecessarily translates *die Frage* with the deictic "*these* words."

19. The respectful distance of the third person is undercut by Strachey's "Are you a doctor, sir?" The distant formality of the Austrian expression is somewhat strained when given a word-for-word rendering; yet I would rather be faulted for a stilted rendering than for neglecting the psychological importance of the deictic.

want to relate it to myself. The question however was intended for me and came[20] from the girl of perhaps eighteen who had served me. . . . Recovering my self-awareness, I answered, "Yes, I am a doctor. Where do you know that from?"[21]

"The gentleman[22] wrote his name in the visitors' book, and then[23] I thought to myself, if the gentleman doctor[24] now[25] might have a little bit of time . . . " So there [*da*] I was again in neuroses . . .

(184–85/125; my translation)

No longer distracted, Freud invited Katharina to sit near him and started to plot spatial and temporal coordinates that would circumscribe her spatial anguish, introduce order into her temporal confusion, and define his own position:

I report the conversation now[26] that occurred between us. . . .

"Sit down here [*her*]. Describe to me how it is when you are in 'need of breath.'"

"It comes suddenly over me . . . I think always, now[27] I will die. Otherwise I'm brave, I go about [*hin*] everywhere alone, in the cellar and away down [*hinunter*] over the whole mountain. But on such a day when that happens, then I don't trust myself away [*hin*] any-

20. Another deictic omitted by Strachey.

21. The deictic sense of *woher* is neutralized by Strachey's "how."

22. Strachey uses "you" and "your."

23. Omitted by Strachey.

24. Strachey substitutes "you."

25. Omitted by Strachey.

26. Omitted by Strachey.

27. Omitted by Strachey.

where; I always think someone is standing behind me
and suddenly grabs me. . . . Yes, I always see such a
horrible face, looking at me in a frightening way, so
that I'm frightened before that."

Perhaps a quick way was then [*da*][28] offering itself
to penetrate to the heart of the matter. . . .

"Do you know where your attacks come from
[*woher*]?"[29]

"No."

"When did you first have them then?"

"For the first time two years ago, when I was still
on the other mountain with my aunt. Earlier she had a
refuge hut there [*dort*], and now we're here [*hier*] since
a year and a half. But they always keep coming."[30]

Was I to make an attempt at an analysis here
[*hier*]?[31] Surely I did not dare to transplant hypnosis to
these [*diese*] altitudes.   (185–86/126–27; my translation)

Let us now widen our focus on the deictics used by
Freud as interlocutor with Katharina to include those used
by him as narrator to the reader. Once more, the importance of a nuanced translation comes into play. Freud in
the German text of his case histories often employs the
present tense, whereby he re-presents himself, the patient,
and the reader; Strachey, however, uses the past tense, thus
ushering into the whole English text a temporal and per-

28. Cf. Strachey's "Perhaps this might offer a quick way of
getting . . ."

29. Cf. Strachey's "Do you know what your attacks come
from?"

30. Cf. Strachey's spatially neutral "happening."

31. In the context a weighty word indeed, but not rendered by
Strachey.

sonal displacement. In other words, Strachey displaces into the historical narration of the past what Freud has restaged in the present. In this same present tense Freud often unites his prior contact with his patient and future rapport with his readers so that the difference between description and event is minimized; Strachey, on the other hand, wants to underscore their disparity. The time is ripe for some clarifying examples.

In relating that he exhorted Katharina to try free association, Freud aptly switches to the present tense as a way of rendering the immediacy of her efforts. (This immediacy is somewhat deadened in Strachey's translation, which drops into the past tense.) The following translation is mine: "She now describes how at last she reported her discovery to her aunt, who found her changed and suspected a secret behind it. . . . Then her aunt decided to move with her children and niece and take over the present inn. . . . Then, to my astonishment, she drops these threads and begins to relate . . . " (189/129).

Another example is equally revelatory in a different way: after using verbal tenses in a quite regular fashion, Freud suddenly resorts to a usage with an anomalous pattern. The subject is the nakedness of the copulating couple, and we suspect some libidinal interference leaving its trace in the temporal distancing and rapprochement in Freud's report. (This point holds even though one may change tenses much more often in German than in English.) In my translation I have underlined the significant tenses:

> So I *said:* "If you were sick three days later, I believe that means that when you looked into the room you felt disgusted."

"Yes, I'm sure I felt disgusted," she *says*[32] reflectively, "but disgusted at what?"

"Perhaps you saw something naked? What sort of state were they in?"

"It was too dark to see anything; besides, both of them had their clothes on. Oh, if only I knew what it was I felt disgusted at!"

I *had* no idea either. But I *told* her to go on and tell me whatever *occurred* to her, in the confident expectation that she would think of precisely what I needed to explain the case.

Well, she *describes*[33]. . . (189/129)

Reflecting further on Freud's use of deictics, we come upon a startling difference: with the help of such linguistic means, the abstemious Freud takes readily to establishing Katharina's story and fixing a therapeutic framework between himself and her. But when his narrative formulas are aimed at the reader as primary audience, and when the text switches from report to commentary, he is apt in various minute ways to loosen his control of deictics. It is as if, given the real temporal and spatial distance involved in writing up the recollected scene, Freud permitted himself to leave some traces of his own impulsive fluctuation.

Let us pursue this topic from yet another angle. Freud words his reflective interruptions of the ensuing dialogue in such a way that they are simultaneously past reflections addressed to himself and present ones shared with the reader as needed confidant (imitative of Katharina's choice of Freud as confidant). A small segment serves to illustrate this engaging procedure (translations partially mine):

32. Strachey: "said."
33. Strachey: "went on to describe."

"I think all the time someone's standing behind me and going to catch hold of me all at once."

So in fact it was an anxiety attack, and introduced by signs of a hysterical "aura"[34]—or, more correctly, it was a hysterical attack the content of which was anxiety. Might there not probably be some other content as well? (186/126)

"When you have an attack do you think of something? and always the same thing? or do you see something in front of you?"

"Yes. I always see an awful face that looks at me in a dreadful way, so that I'm frightened."

Perhaps a quick way was then offering itself to penetrate to the heart of the matter. (186/126)

"But I was so frightened that I've forgotten everything." (Translated into the terminology of our "Preliminary Communication," this means: "The affect itself created a hypnoid state, whose products were then cut from associative connection with the ego-consciousness). (188/128)

"It was too dark in the room. And why should he have been making such a dreadful face just then?"

"You're quite right."

(Then the way seemed suddenly blocked. Perhaps something can be found[35] in the rest of her story.)

(188/128)

34. This term, which Freud immediately corrects, was undoubtedly Freud's klang association to Katharina's real first name, Aurelia (derived, of course, from the Latin *aura*). The klang association is one of the many evidences of Freud's writing being carried out under impulse and influenced by primary process.

35. Cf. Strachey's translation: "was" (p. 132).

These excerpts allow us to perceive how Freud negotiates between his sympathy with Katharina and his proximity to us as readers, permitting us a view of his ongoing suspicions, admissions, and so forth.

As Freud proceeds in his exposition, however, the nature of his interpolated commentary changes. Its character as a reported self-reflection occurring in the past lessens and it becomes mainly interpretable as a subsequent address to the reader: "I have been obliged to relate this event in detail because it possesses a great importance for the understanding of everything coming later. . . . Thus the case would seem cleared up.—But stop a moment! What about the recurrent hallucination of the head?" (190–92/130–32; my translation). In this passage we cannot fail to notice a striking parallel within the story's double movement from private to public. In much the same way that Freud forsook his meditativeness to speak with Katharina, so his private reflections within the narration diminish nature to become more readily interpretable as retrospections addressed to the reader.[36] Thus the clear emergence into public discourse comes to the fore.

My detailed analyses up to now prompt me to make a series of generalizations and nuances. A prominent feature of Freud's style is a common vocabulary that circulates among and unites various areas of reference; this feature I have elsewhere described as the "avoidance of lexical

36. In narratological terms, Freud's text presents some difficulty in disentangling fabula or story from plot; in other words, disengaging the set of narrated situations in chronological sequence from the rearrangement that is presented to the reader.

apartheid" (Mahony 1986). The commonality that Freud finds throughout diverse realms of experience adds to the universal appeal of his prose. Some of that commonality, to be sure, results from Freud's prolonged reflection and thus may be found in his dogmatic discourse—a ready instance is his use of the same vocabulary in his delineation of the normal and the psychopathological in order to indicate their continuity. We surmise that on other occasions, the unity found among Freud's different frames of reference is a more subtle one, due to unconsciously or preconsciously determined use of a common vocabulary. Such an evocative feature typifies Freud's genetic discourse and gives it a poetic force.

We are familiar with creative writers' resorting to a lexical motif to bind scene, agent, action, narrator, reader, and so on. Such a motif cuts across material and psychical reality, creating mutual allusion among their elements. The sexual motif that pervades Katharina's case history, even into its vertical references, is a manifestation of Freud's creative talent as well as his libidinal involvement with his patient. We could even say that the vitality of Freud's genetic style comes in large measure from its responsiveness to his affectivity and associative processes. Freud's employment of deictics is another matter. He could enlist them in the service of therapeutic control, thus striving to contain both his own and Katharina's unsettlement and to promote both an appropriate empathy and a distanced perspective. But when the primary audience entertained by Freud is the readership, he may indulge in a more supple use of deictics. He is aided by the fact that tense shifting is easier in German than in English. Nevertheless, Freud's tendency to restage in the present does not arise merely from an arbitrary preference for the dramatic quality of the historical present. His use of the present also testifies to the power of his imagination to visualize events in the present in a dreamlike way. His imagination is enhanced by his willingness to write under the influence of intense emotion.

Another enlightening perspective may be achieved by viewing the structure of Katharina's case history. The first, narrative part is genetic both in its retracing of a former investigative path and in its exposition of an ongoing investigation: one narrative thread deals with the interaction of Freud the therapist with Katharina; the other deals with Freud's involvement with the reader. Crisscrossing both of these threads are Freud's reflections, which become gradually more public and directly shared with his reader-audience as a hearer rather than an overhearer. Hence, true to complex narrative form, the series of Katharina's staggered reactions to her final traumatic scene is revealed nonlinearly in the multiple stages of her interview with Freud, and interwoven through these are Freud's reflections on the mountaintop and afterward at his writing desk.

Genetic discourse is that part of Freud's writing, as writing, that appeals to us most; it takes on a noticeable charm in the case history of Katharina. The German reader will heed Freud's conversational gesture to shorten Katharina's name (he called her "Katharin'") and to render her dialect, a familiar feature of fictional verisimilitude far removed from the climate of scientific prose. We all can readily delight in Freud's visual style, vivid presentation, and deft handling of scientific terms at the outset so that they do not distract the reader from the vacation setting. We enjoy too the story's opening, so typical of nineteenth-century fiction, and we are amused to hear in the second sentence the echo of the fictional detective who suddenly finds his well-earned vacation interrupted and sees himself once more plunged into the urgent, ubiquitous concerns of his professional life (see Rohner 1966; Schönau 1968, pp. 209–12). Last but not least, there is a powerful aesthetic appeal in the imagery, vertical and other, which is disseminated through various frames of reference and which establishes a commonality in them.

From a compositional point of view, the discussion or second part of the case history is largely in a dogmatic mold—I say largely, for even here there is some genetic discourse that gives evidence of Freud's "writing through" his ideas. For example, after postulating a difference between a splitting of consciousness due to ignorance and one due to conscious rejection, Freud immediately rejects it, questioning the sexual innocence of pubertal juveniles. After calling Katharina's early erotic experiences (her father's attempts at incest) traumatic in comparison to the later "auxiliary" one at sixteen (her discovery of her father and Franziska), he goes on to label the latter as also traumatic. In such procedures, Freud first distinguishes (cf. the etymology of *analysis*, a taking apart) and then collapses the differences into a fundamental similarity. One may suspect here that however much Freud concluded with such unity by rational means, he was to some degree influenced by the thrust of his creative imagination, which, through the dispersion of similar images, united different realms of reference. Briefly, in the case history of Katharina, two kinds of lexical practice produce unity. The most impressive and dominant one is a *dispersion* of similarity and unity; playing a patently subordinate role is the reactive gesture of returning to proposed logical distinctions and *collapsing* them.

The case history of Katharina is actually the report of a random encounter far above sea level. Like any therapist, Freud obviously knew much more than is contained in his report. The selective historical supplement included here enables us to share some of the information that Freud used for his diagnosis but that he refrained from printing; the historical data, together with Freud's and contemporary clinical analyses, help us further to understand his overdetermined reaction during the mountaintop interview and its deferred impact on him when he wrote up the case. In effect, eroticization extended beyond Freud's reported interchange and seeped into his "objective" language. The major portion of the case history is a narrative and hence qualifies as genetic discourse; but even there the narrative is double, for it also relates Freud's ongoing reflections at the time of writing. The language of Freud's narrative or genetic discourse is both evocative and overdetermined; even some of the deictics, which may act as devices of reflective control, appear to be overdetermined. We have also seen that the dogmatic discourse of the discussion contains some evidence of a spontaneous "writing through."

In the next chapter we shall have the chance to discover a very different kind of genetic discourse; if it lacks some of the appealing features of familiar narrative, it yet has a distinctive lexical dynamics. The text is "Analysis Terminable and Interminable," the last word of whose title desgnates that supreme quality Freud found in true genetic discourse . . .

3

Psychoanalysis at Dusk: Analysis Terminable and Interminable

The standard context for the scrutiny and appreciation of "Analysis Terminable and Interminable" is provided in Ernest Jones's (1957, vol. 3, chaps. 4–6) biography of Freud, M. Schur's biography (1970, chaps. 22–27), and the pertinent correspondence in *Letters of Sigmund Freud* (1960) and *The Letters of Sigmund Freud and Arnold Zweig* (1971). Rather than rehash those sources, I will say that with the complete release, on a date as yet undetermined, of all the pertinent primary sources, our contextual comprehension will be enriched. The writings of Anna Freud, Marie Bonaparte, and Minna Bernays will be of decisive importance. Meanwhile I shall content myself with bringing to the fore a number of other, currently available texts.

The most thorough study of Freud's struggle with cancer is *The Unwelcome Intruder* (1983), the result of a year's research by the plastic surgeon Sharon Romm. In 1936, a year before the publication of "Analysis Terminable and Interminable," the cancer-stricken Freud, attended to by a

trio of doctors—Max Schur, Hans Pichler, and Jakob Erd-
heim—underwent several surgical interventions. Romm
describes Freud's medical history in 1936 as follows:

> On January 4, Schur noticed a wart-like prominence,
> coarse and papillomatous, which had grown with
> alarming speed over the preceding two weeks. Because
> there was no palpable hardening of the area, Pichler
> felt there was a remote chance that it was not a malig-
> nancy and it might be prudent to follow the conser-
> vative course of observation.
>
> In the spring, recurrent and persistent leuko-
> plakias became a source of trouble, and Pichler re-
> sorted to various methods of attacking the lesions short
> of operation. . . . Nonetheless, in July Freud had no
> choice but to submit to yet another operation. This
> time Erdheim personally telephoned Pichler to inform
> him that the specimen he had examined undeniably
> contained squamous cell carcinoma; this was the first
> documented cancerous recurrence since the initial ex-
> cision in 1923. . . . This dreaded diagnosis also had a
> ring of finality. Freud had lived 13 years without the
> cancer declaring its presence. Now, however, the vigil
> had to be maintained in the knowledge that any day
> further malignant and potentially lethal lesions might
> appear. . . . As the year ended, Freud was still in con-
> stant pain, and his general condition seemed to be
> weakening. . . . [In December] during an excision and
> electrocoagulation of an ulcer in a location both poorly
> accessible and particularly difficult to anesthetize,
> Freud said that he could simply stand no more. (pp.
> 106–107)

This information about Freud's physical and affective
state up to December 1936 proves extremely useful, for, as
the dated first page of my photocopy of the holograph of
"Analysis Terminable and Interminable" shows, Freud

was busy with its composition on 18 January 1937.[1] The holograph contains a number of corrections, the major one being that the first three lines on page 19, as well as the number 19 itself, are repeated and crossed out at the top of page 21. From this indication one may conjecture that Freud set about composing his essay in January and on the eighteenth of that month quickly began writing the definitive version. I should like to bring this chronology into a most astounding relation that has hitherto been neglected by critics—the return of the suppressed and perhaps even partially repressed Fliess connection.

The story goes as follows. On 30 December 1936, Marie Bonaparte wrote to Freud that his correspondence with Fliess had survived and that she was about to purchase it from a dealer. The news from Bonaparte jolted Freud, and he replied immediately on 3 January:

> The matter of the correspondence with Fliess has affected me deeply. . . . Our correspondence was the most intimate you can imagine. It would have been highly embarrassing to have it fall into the hands of strangers. . . . May I offer to share half the cost with you? After all, I would have had to acquire the letters

---

1. Strachey merely notes that the paper was written early in 1937 and then published in June (*SE* 23:211). Jones (1957, p. 213) mistakenly finds a reference to the paper's exposition in the following excerpt from Freud's letter to Max Eitingon on February 5, 1937: "A brief technical essay which is slowly taking shape has the function of helping me fill the many free hours with which my dwindling analytical practice has presented me" (Freud 1961, p. 431). My own conclusions are that after "Analysis Terminable" was written up in January, Freud in the next month turned to "Constructions in Analysis"—this, in fact, was the "brief technical essay . . . slowly taking shape."

myself if the man had approached me directly. I do not
want any of them to become known to so-called pos-
terity.   (Freud 1985, p. 7)

The impact of the extant correspondence was so painful,
Anna Freud declared, that her father spoke about it to her
only very sparingly until the end of his life (Freud 1985, p.
4). This becomes all the more understandable when we
realize that for most of his mature years, Freud's close rela-
tionships were with two men, Jung and Ferenczi, who in
their imaginative flair reminded him very much of Fliess
(Mahony 1979a, pp. 87–89; 1979b, 558–59). Might one
say that the interminability of Freud's transference onto
Fliess flowed through the penning of "Analysis Terminable"?

Also bearing on the composition of Freud's essay were
dogs. On December 6, 1936, Freud wrote to thank Marie
Bonaparte for her book *Topsy*, named after her pet chow.
(In the same letter, incidentally, the eighty-year-old Freud
wondered if he would last another year, until the age his
father and half-brother Emmanuel had died.) Bonaparte
wrote the book to commemorate her dog's favorable response to treatment for a cancer of the oral cavity; her
touching account refers to a number of other topics, including her father's painful death from cancer. For more or less
obvious reasons the book pleased Freud. Eleven days later,
he wrote to her again, this time about his own dog: "I wish
you could have seen what sympathy Jo-fi shows me in my
suffering, just as if she understood everything." Freud
stated his fondness of dogs since they, in contrast to human
beings, lack ambivalence; Freud's desire for canine com-
panionship, we may speculate, may also have arisen from a
dog's particular facility for being invested with multiple

identifications—child, partner, parent—either alternately or simultaneously. On 12 January, twelve days before Freud drew up the final version of "Analysis Terminable and Interminable," the affectionate dog that he had known for nearly seven years died during an operation for ovarian cysts. In light of his mournful feelings for his own dog, Freud began translating Bonaparte's commemorative volume in August of the same year. Anna Freud portrayed the mood of the translator:

> Today we may assume that it was not only the person of the author but, above all, the topic of the book which influenced Freud's choice. What at that time, perhaps as never before, made for disappointment were people. Even the destruction of illusions during the First World War could not measure up to the impressions of unrelenting brutality and blind lust for destruction which no one could escape. Instinctual manifestations which, according to Freud, should have been banished to the unconscious and warded off by the higher agencies of the personality, suddenly emerged, unleashed and unrestricted in their search for gratification. In these circumstances it became easier to look away from one's fellow men and turn to animals.[2]

2. For the material in this paragraph I am indebted to Jones (1957, pp. 210–11, 224); Schur (1972, p. 491); Anna Freud (1980, pp. 359–60); and last but not least, Bonaparte's moving story of *Topsy* (1936). Lynne Reiser's recent article is a superb examination of the book's further importance (Reiser 1987). In an interesting sidelight on the volume, Bonaparte disclosed to Freud that her lover, for whom "the father [was] taboo," tormented her about any allusion she made to her own father's lethal disease (Bertin 1982, p. 314). Another pertinent point is that during this period Marie Bonaparte had a reactively intensified caninophilia similar to Freud's (Bertin 1982, pp. 310, 314).

We can now quickly sum up the context of "Analysis Terminable and Interminable." Its unforgettable background gives us every reason to linger. Looming over Europe were successful fascist abominations and the terror of Nazism, a caricature of all that ever was and could be human. (The interminable invincibility of the totalitarian forces of Nazism and fascism comes from the fact that their atrocities defy description in human language.) Political, social, and economic turmoil disrupted Central Europe—Freud had every cause to doubt whether his scientific child, psychoanalysis, would survive. A drumroll of less public factors also contributed to Freud's gloom: painful awareness of his ebbing creativity, the ravaging debilitation of terminal disease amplified by numerological superstitions about the amount of life remaining to him, the death of his comforting dog, and the sudden reemergence of his intimate letters to Fliess. In addition, Freud was experiencing a certain disaffection with his lifelong wife (Clark 1980, p. 483), while around him he saw psychoanalysis increasingly beset with difficulties: defections of close collaborators multiplied, and Freud even felt deserted by Felix and Helene Deutsch and the many others who left to practice in America, the land he had so long disdained; he also complained to Lou Andreas-Salomé that many of his colleagues had "derived little from analysis as far as their personal character is concerned" (6 Jan. 1935, Freud 1966, p. 204). Attendantly, there was the growing roll of patients who bore the worrisome effects of long analysis—most notably the Wolf Man, who began treatment with Freud in 1910 and from 1926 on was in and out of analysis with Ruth Mack Brunswick, who herself was in and out of treatment with Freud from 1926 on and was resorting to dangerous drugs during the 1930s (Bertin 1982, p. 354). Nor must we forget Marie Bonaparte, who, intermittently in analysis with Freud from 1925 to 1938 (Roudinesco 1982, p. 332), fancifully tried to cure her frigidity by undergoing two vain operations to move her clitoris nearer her urethral meatus. She saw her former lover Loewenstein take her son into analysis in 1930, and she herself went into analysis with Loewenstein for a while in 1932 (Bertin 1982, pp. 180, 186–87). Anna Freud was analyzed by her father from 1918 to 1922 and from 1924 to 1925; her persistent spinsterhood gave rise to his fatherly concern.

This disquieting context gives us a better appreciation of Freud's resolute scientific commitment to take a stand against the optimistic position of the symposium on "The Theory of Therapeutic Results" held at the fourteenth International Psychoanalytic Congress in 1936. "Analysis Terminable and Interminable" was the last great text Freud completed, and more than any other work in his corpus it demonstrates his courage. Admirers are wont to allude to Freud's determination during his period of "splendid isolation" in the 1890s and especially his unsettling switch from a literal acceptance of reports of childhood traumas to an explanation of them and their hysterical sequelae as fantasy. If Freud triumphed in that period of isolation, he achieved an even greater triumph forty years later, when he underwent a different kind of isolation, awful, not splendid, which moved inside and which he stoically confronted—"a small island of pain floating on an ocean of indifference."[3] Out of this later

3. Although this quotation is drawn from a letter of 16 July 1939 to Marie Bonaparte, its larger context has a retrospective import: "*and my world is what it was previously:* a small island of pain

isolation, I believe, arose a creativity more intriguing than anything before it, involving a reversal in the opposite direction: the fantasy of early cures giving way to the reality of endless psychoanalysis.

We cannot mistake the bitter irony of a man named Sigmund (lit., victory-mouth) whose mouth was wracked by scar and torment and who could see before him only numbered days of physical agony, nevertheless courageously taking up arms against the shortening of the analytic process. The unique achievement of Freud's genius, I believe, is determined by four components: raw intellectual power, imaginative creativity, a supreme linguistic endowment, and not least, courage.[4] There have been many intellectual giants in history, but how many of these equalled Freud in courage? To understand the indispensability of such courage for the composition of "Analysis Terminable and Interminable," let us turn to those darkest of days when the father, fending off his daughter's suggestion of family suicide, defiantly replied, "Why? Because they would like us to?" (Schur 1972, p. 499).

Coming to closer terms with Freud's text, we realize only too well that it shares the limitations of its time. At the same time we can only imagine the additions and modifications that Freud would bring to the text if he were revising it today: preoedipal and postoedipal developmental issues,

---

floating on an ocean of indifference" (Schur 1972, p. 524, italics mine).

4. See Freud's letter of 4 April 1915 to Ferenczi: "Let me admit that I have found in myself only one attribute of first quality: a kind of courage that is not affected by conventions" (Jones 1955, p. 183). See also Jones (1955, pp. 424–427, 431, 433); Eissler (1971, p. 307).

sexual and gender identity, structural aspects of the ego and its nondefensive complexity, the manifold elements in defensive functioning, the formation and aims of the super-ego, differences in traumatic etiology, the role of mourning and reparation, narcissistic and borderline pathology, termination as a phase of treatment, the pervasiveness of negative transference, the complications of countertransference, and so on.[5]

As a text, "Analysis Terminable and Interminable" is largely genetic in that it proceeds in an unfolding way. It is also mimetic, not only addressing textually the dogmatic position of analytic endlessness closure announced in the Marienbad Congress but enacting self-reflectively its style. Freud talked about process in a processive way. Here are several examples of his thinking aloud in this manner:

> I throw out these questions without proposing to answer them now. Perhaps it may not be possible at present to give any certain answer to them at all. Some light may probably be thrown on them by theoretical considerations. . . . An analytic experience which now extends over several decades, and a change which has taken place in the nature and mode of my activity, encourage me to attempt to answer the questions before us. (pp. 223–24)

> It is not in our power to awaken them [sleeping dogs]. This last statement does not seem to be quite accurate and calls for a more detailed discussion. (p. 231)

> It soon becomes evident . . . (p. 250)[6]

5. For lengthier enumerations, see Anzieu (1987), Berenstein (1987), and especially Arlow (1987), Blum (1987), and Cooper (1987).
6. Single page numbers refer to Freud's essay in volume 23 of

Processive though it may be, "Analysis Terminable and Interminable" is not a faultless achievement. The contextual influence of social and personal disturbances traced by critics undoubtedly bore also on the essay's organizational slackness. "Analysis Terminable and Interminable" lacks the impressive architectonic design of Freud's other associative works, *The Interpretation of Dreams* (1900), *Beyond the Pleasure Principle* (1920), and *Civilization and Its Discontents* (1930) (Mahony 1987). In the loose design of "Analysis Terminable and Interminable," radial connections predominate over lateral ones: each of the essay's eight sections connects with its title and elaborates on a core problem related to it, but the connections between sections and the transitions from one section to another are rather uneven. The first section deals with attempts to speed up analytic treatment and hence make it terminable. In sections 2–7 the problem takes on an interrogatory character marked by the recurrence of the word *Frage* (question) and its variants (*fragen, befragen, Fragestellung*); thus the essay's central portion becomes an entangled forest of evergreen questions. The second section treats the question of whether there is a natural end to analysis, suggests the possibility of an end when the psychic disorder is due to trauma rather than to drive strength or ego alteration, and then ends up with three questions which will occupy the next two sections.

The first of those questions, whether conflict can be resolved permanently, is considered in the light of drive

---

the *Standard Edition*. Two numbers separated by a slash refer to the *Gesammelte Werke* (vol. 16) and to the *Standard Edition* (vol. 23) respectively.

strength in section 3. The other two questions are reformulated in section 4: can we successfully treat a conflict that is not current? This section is the most difficult of all to follow as Freud becomes needlessly enmeshed in his categories. It is perhaps for this reason that at the beginning of section 5 Freud summarizes what he has covered so far; the rest of the section examines the question of acquired ego alteration. Section 6 starts with the subject of congenital ego alterations but then veers off into an examination of the drives. The theme of section 7, the psychoanalyst's recurrent need for treatment, does not fit well with the surrounding context and, in terms of logical exigency, should have come last. On the other hand, the final section, which examines the analytic bedrock of bisexuality and castration, is only very loosely connected with the matter of sections 6 and 7.

If the general structure of "Analysis Terminable and Interminable" is slack and if this may be partly explained by the historical and personal disorder in Freud's life, particular structural disturbance of the essay's first and last sections demand supplementary explanation.[7] It is as if each end of the essay has a reversed parenthesis—a mark of punctuation unable to contain the essay that opens with

7. Evidences of thematic disquiet in Freud's text are many. He draws unprecedented attention to biological and physical factors largely outside the bounds of psychological influence; he refers to the superego on only one page; to cite a minor example, several animals anecdotally mentioned share in adding to the stark tone: the baby-bringing stork is outnumbered by the springing lion, the dangerous sleeping dog, and the primeval dragon. But overriding any pessimism were Freud's scientific and human concerns, which prompted him to publish his thoughts in the first place.

stories about shortening analysis and ends by referring to a developmental bedrock that eludes full analysis. Furthermore, although one might think that Freud starts his essay suitably by discussing Otto Rank's experiments in the New World, that story is overdetermined, lacks Freud's usually complete expository control, and points to incompletely analyzed material in his own life. Freud's allegation that Rank began his accelerated treatments in America is not true—Rank began experimenting with shortened analyses in 1921, and at least two months before Rank left for America, in April 1924, Freud had discussed Rank's new theoretical and technical orientation in a circular letter to the secretly governing psychoanalytic committee (Jones 1957, pp. 58–67; Lieberman 1985, p. 215). Freud's falsification makes sense in terms of his extraordinary ambivalence toward the United States, especially after his trip to Clark University. On the one hand, he was grateful that he had received his first public recognition in America; there he had realized an "incredible daydream" (Freud 1925, p. 52). On the other hand, Freud attributed a host of his physical symptoms, including chronic constipation and even bad handwriting, to his American experience. Yet we know that constipation affected Freud throughout his life and was distressingly active for many years prior to his voyage across the Atlantic (Jones 1955, pp. 59–60, 391–92).

At the antipodes to the New World in section 1 is the bedrock (*gewachsener Fels;* lit., mature rock) in section 8. Here Freud contests Fliess's conception of bisexuality but nowhere recognizes his theoretical indebtedness to Fliess; the recent reemergence of the Fliess letters seems to have reactivated Freud's and Fliess's conflict over priority in the theoretical discovery of bisexuality (Mahony 1979a, pp. 78–89). Thus "Analysis Terminable and Interminable" contains not even the slightest hint of Freud's acknowledgment in the *Three Essays:* "Since I have been acquainted through Wilhelm Fliess with the notion of bisexuality, I have regarded it as the decisive factor" (Freud 1905b, p. 220). It is of significance that Freud twice uses *gewachsener Fels* instead of the suitable, allied term *Muttergestein* (lit., mother rock). This unnamed element, I suggest, constitutes the lowest layer in Freud's own unanalyzed bedrock.

In the holograph, the final section is not separated off but rather constitutes the final part of the seventh section.[8] In this version, then (in keeping with the numerological superstitions about death that plagued him in 1936 and 1937), Freud had given to his essay the sevenfold organization that characterized many of his writings. This organization had unconscious determinants. The first of the two parts of the Rat Man case has a heptadic organization, as do the following:

> *The Interpretation of Dreams, Jokes and Their Relation to the Unconscious,* "The Unconscious," *New Introductory Lectures, Beyond the Pleasure Principle,* and

8. Was it Freud who emended the printer's proofs by separating off the closing paragraphs with the roman numeral VIII? Additionally, the plural German noun *Relationen* was changed to the singular *Relation* on the proofs (69n/226n), and *beibehalten* (retained) in the holograph was patently changed on the proofs to *anerkannt* (recognized, 71/221). Such emendations may have been made by the printer without consulting Freud; or perhaps they were made by Anna, who may have mentioned them to her father.

> *The Question of Lay Analysis. . . . The Introductory
> Lectures* are twenty-eight in number [thus a multiple
> of seven]; the first two of the *Three Essays on the The-
> ory of Sexuality* have seven sections each, as does
> Freud's personal favorite among all his writings, Part
> Four of *Totem and Taboo.* Relatedly, Freud thought
> his life was marked by seven-year cycles; he specifi-
> cally linked seven to a prediction of death and the
> effort of his seven internal organs to usher his life to
> an end; and he eventually visited the forbidden city of
> Rome and its seven hills for a total of seven times
> after having phobically avoided it for years (Mahony
> 1986, pp. 186–87).

In "Analysis Terminable and Interminable," the fact
that the seventh and eighth sections in no way belong together makes the heptadic organization in the final holograph all the more significant in terms of Freud's unending
numerological superstition, which was inscribed into the
very composition of an essay about interminable analysis,
thus making the essay a piece of enactive discourse that
demonstrates itself.

Discursively, the lexical skill manifest in Freud's essay
is its most distinctive characteristic and serves to offset its
sprawling, unstrung organization. Since the artistic traces
of Freud's master hand over polyvalent verbal usage are
many, I shall start off with some incidental features, which
will slowly prepare us for the essential. Here and there in
the essay, intermingling with oracular phrases that are un-
expectedly echoed from our own lips in conversation, we
come upon light-tongued ironies, some that even show a
bewitching mix of avowal and denial; for example, observe
Freud as he resorts to justifications: "We can only say: '*So*

muss denn doch die Hexe dran!'—the Witch Metapsy-
chology. Without metapsychological speculation and the-
orizing—I had almost said 'phantasying'—we shall not get
another step forward" (p. 225). The appreciative reader
needs even more agility to keep in step with Freud as he
ironically plays tag with valid generalizations: "We know
that the first step towards attaining intellectual mastery of
our environment is to discover generalizations, rules and
laws which bring order into chaos. . . . A shrewd satirist of
old Austria, Johann Nestroy, once said: 'Every step forward
is only half as big as it looks at first.' It is tempting to
attribute a quite general validity to this malicious dictum"
(p. 228).

These examples of metacommentary folded into commentary are paralleled by several interesting cases of random punning—which fortunately have escaped accusations
of recklessness by some scientific purists (oedipal wrecks,
one might reckon). At one point Freud playfully hopes that
the beneficial stimuli the analyst receives in his own analysis
do not come to a stop when it ends—the English word *stop*
does not convey the German *Aufhören*, which literally
means "hearing off" (87/238). Elsewhere Freud wryly indicates that the strengthened adult ego, defending itself
against imagined dangers (*Gefahren*), compulsively seeks
out situations which "almost replace the original danger"
(*die ursprüngliche Gefahr ungefähr ersetzen*, 83/238); here
the brilliant linguistic effect comes from *ungefähr* (almost),
etymologically cousin to *Gefahr* (danger) and phonetically
similar to it, fittingly used to qualify the substitute danger as
an approximate one. Earlier, Freud pictures the ambitious
analyst who presumes that he "has driven his influence on

the patient so far (*die Beeinflussung des Patienten soweit getrieben hat*) that no further change can be entertained" (63/219). To follow Freud's undercutting of such therapeutic ambitiousness, one should notice his suggestive use of "drive" in its verbal form.

It does not take much textual scrutiny to find other, more involved or more striking examples of Freud's attainment of implicative force by putting aside the difference between language and metalanguage. Let us exemplify and examine this textual feature in an enumerated series whose length is justified by its import:

1. In the original German, Freud asserts the commonality between the woman's strongest motive, penis envy, which "pushed" (*gedrängt*) her into treatment, and the end of our therapeutic efforts, when they have "pushed through" (*durchgedrungen*) to that deepest psychological bedrock, penis envy (the related verbs *drängen* and *durchdringen* are diversely rendered by Strachey as "come" and "penetrate": 99/252).

2. When dealing with Rank's ideas, Freud offers us an activated field of lexically blended commentary and metacommentary. Hence we are told that Rank's theory of birth trauma is "born of its time" (*aus der Zeit geboren*, 60/216), "conceived" (*konzipiert*) under contrasting conditions, and designed to adjust the rhythm of therapy to the rapid tempo of American life. Writing from the vantage point of the Great Depression, Freud adds that Rank's accelerated experimentation and American "prosperity" are things of the past. In asserting that Rank's theory of birth trauma is itself marked by birth and even conception, Freud uses a German verb which, like its English translation *conceived*,

means "apprehended" as well as "become pregnant." Then, to underscore the aberration of Rank's therapy, Freud twice links it with America, a foreign land whose "prosperity" is wryly referred to by this English word, set off by both italics and quotation marks, hence a triple textual alienation from the surrounding context. As if this were not enough, Freud leads up to Rank's accelerated therapy with the brilliantly mimetic exhortation that it be "disposed of as quickly as possible."

3. A short while later Freud goes on to say that occasionally a treatment must be unilaterally terminated by the analyst even though no general rule is available "as to the right for resorting to this forcible device." Strachey's Freud then continues, "the decision must be left to the analyst's tact. A miscalculation cannot be rectified. The saying that a lion only springs once must apply here" (p. 219). Actually the English word "tact" exposes but one meaning of the German *Takt*, which also refers to musical time or measure. Thus Freud is saying that the decision to terminate must be left to the analyst's tact about tact and timing and tact about timing. "Miscalculation" is likewise not adequate to the German *Misgriff*, whose literal meaning, "erroneous grasp" anticipates the kinesthetic notes of the next sentence, translated closely as, "The saying that the lion springs only once necessarily takes hold here" (*muss recht behalten*).

4. In his discussion of the famous Empedocles, with whom he identified, Freud introduced a motif of replication which pervades different frames of reference. Preoccupied by ideas of equality and precedence, Freud mentions both his contemporaries and his predecessors. He first

states that his new dual theory of the drives as "equally authorized partners" (*gleichberechtigten Partner*, 90/244) will find "concord" (*Anklang*) among fellow analysts. Then after declaring that he "found our theory again" (*wiederfand*) in Empedocles' writings, he wonders whether in fact he has succumbed to cryptomnesia. "Found again," of course, is an ambiguous phrase; it could mean that the theory was found twice by Freud in Empedocles' works. (This important nuance is eliminated in Strachey's translation, which unjustifiably omits the "again" and attributes the theory to Freud: "Not long ago I came upon this theory of mine in the writings of one of the great thinkers of ancient Greece.")[9] Ending his commentary on Empedocles, Freud diffuses his motif of replication into a series of visual and spatial inner and outer references that are more evident in the German text: "Und niemand kann vorher*sehen, in* welcher *Ein*kleidung der Wahrheits*kern in* der Lehre des Empedokles sich späterer *Einsicht zeigen* wird" ("And no one can foresee in what clothing the core of truth in the theory of Empedocles will show itself to later insight"; 93/247, my translation and italics).

5. Throughout "Analysis Terminable and Interminable" the activities of sleeping and awakening are given a figurative role (Strachey tends to translate *wecken*, to awake, and its variants by "stir" or "arouse"). Formerly claiming to have "disturbed the sleep of the world," the Viennese conquistador was now deep in the evening of his life. Expectably, he was preoccupied with thoughts about

9. An indication of Freud's overdetermined identification with Empedocles is that the most heavily corrected section of the holograph is that on this Greek philosopher.

sleeping and awakening,[10] which he figuratively dissemi-
nates throughout his essay. During sleep, Freud tells us,
the demands of the drives awaken (*Erwachen,* 70/226). In
the clinical scene itself, the analyst's own driven demands
are liable to be "shaken out of sleep" (*wachgerüttelt,*
95/249), where the elements of positive transference ought
to be wakened in the patient (*zu erweckenden,* 84/239). On
the other hand, if conflicts are sleeping, it is not in our
power to awaken them, Freud repeatedly insists (67/223,
75/231, 77–78/233).

6. At one point in section 3 Freud highlights his repeated clarifications of drive strength (*Stärke*) by taking into
consideration the strength (*Stärke*) of a certain objection
(71/227). Later, in the midst of thrice referring to a man's
"repudiation of femininity" (*Ablehnung der Weiblichkeit,*
97–99/250–52), Freud declares that he himself "repudi-
ates" (*ablehne,* 98/251) sexualizing repression in the manner of Fliess.

7. A grander instance of analogical dispersion is found
in Freud's use of the related words *verbunden, binden,
Bündnistreue,* and *bändigen.*[11] In this way Freud binds up
the following four concepts:

- Analysts bind themselves in an alliance with their pa-

10. This is but one of the many temporal elements permeating
Freud's essay; the temporal range stretches from original inanimate
life to animate life to phylogenetic heritage and across the arc of
history to modern analytic treatment, finished, not finished, periodic,
unending. Such a linear progression, however, does not do justice to
Freud's dialectical struggle with time.

11. The usual, accurate translation of *Bändigung*—and one followed by Strachey—is "taming."

tients (*verbünden*, p. 79; cf. Strachey's "ally ourselves," p. 235).
- Our therapeutic effort is bound up with making conscious what is repressed (*gebunden*, p. 84; cf. Strachey's "depends," p. 238).
- The alteration of the ego threatens its bond of loyalty in analytic work (*Bündnistreue*, p. 85; cf. Strachey's "loyalty," p. 239).
- When a person's drives are not strong, he can manage to keep them within bounds (*Bändigung*, p. 70/226; see also 64/220, 69/226).

If the last examples especially show how the diffusion of unifying links operates in Freud's essay, they do not represent the central lexical activity, as do the dispersed vertical images of Katharina's case history. In "Analysis," Freud reserves the principal lexical activity for pairs of words, which he may differentiate and then collapse or undercut. To some degree, then, we are reminded of Freud's cherished joke about the defendant who protested that he had never borrowed the kettle in question; second, the kettle already had a hole when he borrowed it; and third, he had returned the kettle undamaged (Freud 1900, p. 62).

Let us begin with the very binary title of Freud's mature essay, "Die endliche und die unendliche Analyse," which is rather adequately translated as "Analysis Finite and Infinite" (Berenstein 1987, pp. 28–30; Leupold-Löwenthal 1987, pp. 62–63). But even more incisive for our concerns are the translation and accompanying commentary by Helmut Junker (MS):

Note that even in the few exact words of this title an

obvious logical contradiction between terminable *and* interminable is given in the grammatical form of jux-taposition; it is not "either or" but "and." From the very first moment of reading Freud you are caught in a way of thinking that cannot be called scientific (in the sense of true or false), and which burdens you with a claim to questioning, deliberating, not finding a ready-to-hand answer, neither for theory nor for prac-tice. . . .

The connotation of *endlich* can be "ending," "a process of ending," "having ended," "being limited, finite and final"—so how do we translate that term? The term *unendlich* has, in its German connotations transcribed into English, these meanings: "infinite," "boundless," "endless." . . . A convenient literal translation into English would be "the ending and the non-ending analysis," giving a flow, a movement of thought, interwoven and without a chance of logical explication and definition.

I have quoted Junker's brilliant explication at length not only because it is so perceptive but also because it can be amplified and modified. I suggest that we translate the title of Freud's essay as follows: "Analysis, its endingness and unendingness." This pair of nouns best renders the diverse meanings of the German adjectives *endliche* and *un-endliche*, whose various references to time as process or state define the essay. Interacting with the references to process or state, the conjunction *und* (and) means "in addi-tion to" as well as "is similar or equal to" and even assumes the disjunctive force of "or." Hence the sensitive reader, moving through Freud's text, sees these various meanings ricochet off each other; as a tourist cruising through Nor-wegian fjords is struck by the perspectives endlessly changing fore and aft, so the reader of Freud's essay, as often as he or she returns to it, is overwhelmed by his or her ongoing anticipations and retrospections in their unending permutations. And even when this alert reader pauses in his journey, he or she does not come across a still picture; for example, is the analyst who undertakes reanalysis every five years engaged in an ending or a nonending analysis? The *"und"* of Freud's title here clearly tips over into the sense of "is equal to," much as an analytic treatment, viewed as an hourglass, can be considered half full or half empty—dependent on the envisaged ends.

The unending dialectic of Freud's polysemous title interplays with a lengthy series of conjunctive/disjunctive pairs recurring throughout the essay. It is this unloosed syntax and verbal interaction rather than any grand architectonic design that distinguishes Freud's essay. The work contains the continually shifting perspectives of a conceptual mobile. Or an astronomical model might better illustrate the essay: like stellar bodies, the lexical pairs variously move around each other while their larger cyclical movements interlock with those of their serendipitous associates, creating new fields of force. Some examples:

Constitutional and accidental/acquired. Freud uses this lexical pair to begin his discussion of neurotic disturbance, with or without any appreciable ego alteration. He then collapses alternative neurotic etiologies into a combinatory one (the *either-or* immediately becomes *and*), writing, "It is a question *either* of the instincts being excessively strong—that is to say, recalcitrant to taming by the ego—*or* of the effects of early (i.e., premature) traumas which the immature ego was unable to master. As a rule there is a *com-*

bination of both factors, the constitutional *and* the accidental" (p. 220, my italics). Afterward, upon redefining the
notion of constitutional drive strength, Freud momentarily
drops the *and* in relating neurotic etiology strictly to the drives; then he reasserts a dual neurotic etiology but upgrades
the combinatory sense of *and* to a relational one: "Everyday
experience, however," Freud writes, "teaches us that in a
normal person any solution of an instinctual conflict only
holds good for a particular strength of instinct, or, more correctly, only for a particular relation between the strength of
the instinct and the strength of the ego" (pp. 225–26). Arriv-
ing at section 5, Freud turns to the ego and says that its alterations are "either congenital or acquired" (p. 235), only to
collapse that antithesis in section 6: "we must not exaggerate
the difference between inherited and acquired characteristics [of the ego] into an antithesis; what was acquired by
our forefathers certainly forms an important part of what we
inherit" (p. 240).

*Quantitative and qualitative factors in psychic disor-
der.* Beginning with section 2, Freud asserts that the
strength of the drives is not responsible for ego alteration,
which has an etiology of its own (p. 221). From section 3 on,
however, the two independent qualitative and quantitative
factors are seen together, although primacy rather than
equality informs the *and:* quantity and quality are concur-
rent, but the dominance of drive strength can cause ego
alteration (pp. 226, 230, 240). With section 6, though, the
and is put aside: according to Freud, a tendency to conflict
exists "irrespective of the quantity of the libido"; that is,
conflict arises from the qualitative duality of the two primal
drives (p. 244).

Ego and drives/id. The antithesis between the ego and the drives is suddenly redone in section 5 into one between the ego and the id. In section 6, after referring to the original unity of the ego and the id (p. 240), Freud notes that the resistances present in both collapse much of their topographical distinction (p. 241). From there Freud goes on to assert that the primal drives might be found in the ego and superego as well as in the id (p. 242). Finally, he attributes to the Eros the aim to create structures (p. 246)—a far cry from the earlier assertion that ego alterations have an etiology all their own, independent of the drives (p. 221). In this picture it is as if the two substantive entities separated by *and* have been relocated, thus eclipsing the original function of the conjunction.

Biological and psychological. The connection between this lexical pair undergoes a series of changes. First, while carping about Empedocles' failure to distinguish between the inanimate and the animate, Freud points to the "biophysical field," the "biological basis" underpinning his psychological theory of the drives (p. 246). Subsequently, in section 8, Freud states that he refuses to accept Fliess's explanation of repression in that its reliance on antithesis between the sexes is "on biological grounds instead of purely psychological ones" (p. 251). Yet on the next page Freud removes the *instead of* and adds some ground salt to his own purely psychological diet: "The repudiation of femininity can be nothing else than a biological fact."

A few other lexical pairs in the essay can be briefly mentioned. In Freud's estimation the absolute separation between normality and abnormality is but a mere "fiction."

The *and* between the terms explicitly or implicitly becomes a link that readjusts continuity: the ego of every normal person approximates that of a psychotic (pp. 235, 239); a patient in treatment may become healthier than his analyst (p. 247);[12] there is not necessarily a thoroughgoing difference in behavior between an analyzed and an unanalyzed person (p. 228). Another lexical pair is theory and experience or practice, which constitutes Freud's bipolar investigative method (p. 220). Nevertheless, the *and* between the two concepts may indicate a counterproductive complementarity, as in the case of Rank and of children, whose experience and theory prevent them from truly perceiving (pp. 217, 234). But then, in another twist of the

12. To quote Freud: "It cannot be disputed that analysts in their own personalities have not *thoroughly* come up to the standard of psychical normality to which they wish to educate their parents." The word I have translated as "thoroughly" is the German *durchwegs* (*GW* 16:93), which Strachey mistakenly translates as "invariably." Whereas the implication of Strachey's translation is that some analysts do come up to the standard of psychic normality, Freud's claim is more modest and subtle—no analyst has thoroughly fulfilled such a standard. Elsewhere, obviously disagreeing with Freud's calling the analytic patient an "object" (*Objekt*), Strachey three times softens this term to "subject" (65/221, 76/232, 79/235); elsewhere he purges the tautology of *Hochflut der Triebsteigerung* (high tide of instinctual rising, 71/227), rendering it as "rising flood of instinctual strength." His paring down of Freud's literary conception of the clinical encounter is more serious: Strachey's correct translation of the analyst's resort to a "heroic measure" (*heroischen Mittel,* 61/227) is not matched by his rendering of the patient's *Liebesroman* as "romance" in place of the more pointed, literally accurate "love novel" (66/222). The obscuring of Freud's literary theme is even more remarkable in Strachey's translation of the Rat Man case (Mahony 1986).

connective *and,* Freud speaks of a positive divergence between theory and practice in insisting that whatever one's
theoretical attitude may be about the endlessness of analysis, its termination stands as a practical matter in a number
of cases, whereas (a final twist) a conjunctive harmony obtains in character analyses, where "there is a far smaller
discrepancy between theory and practice" (pp. 249–50).

It remains for another lexical pair to carry the burden
of Freud's complex attitude to existence itself: "It is not a
question of an antithesis between an optimistic and pessimistic theory of life," he writes. "Only the primal drives of
Eros and the death drive, in their working together *and*
against each other—and never alone—can explain the variety of the phenomena of life" (88–89/243, translation
and italics mine). The *and* here is not a fixed divider separating independently operating entities but rather a circuit
marker of their interchange.[13] In sum, the interchange typ-
ifying Freud's conception of the drives and his attitude
toward life is figured in a series of lexical pairs so fluidly
connected in his text that they become quasi-neologisms,
going beyond their dictionary univocity to acquire con-
geries of interactive meanings which reflect "the variety of
the phenomena of life."

13. In some ways it is as if Freud leads us back to the world of
jokes where "yes" stands for "no," where "and" can mean "either-
or," or, more radically, where "either-or" does not exist and where
unconsciously there is no room for the "mutual cancelling-out of
several thoughts" (Freud 1905, p. 205; see also pp. 62, 70). Again, the
power of "Analysis Terminable and Interminable" is best seen, not in
any obvious narrative features, but in the logical instability of the key
lexical pairs it deals with.

The global challenge facing Freud the analyst-writer, then, was to aim at the scientific ideal of drawing generalizations founded on particular observations while at the same time doing justice to the specificity of psychic material. The processiveness of this psychic material is distorted by generalizations, for in making them, "we cannot simplify the world of phenomena; but we cannot avoid falsifying it, especially if we are dealing with processes of development and change" (p. 228). To be more precise, the descriptive challenge confronting Freud was double, for the phenomena he dealt with were wont to change gradually and never completely:

> In studying developments and changes we direct our attention to outcomes; we readily overlook the fact that such processes are usually more or less complete—that is to say, that they are in fact only partial alterations. . . . [Phasic] replacements do not take place all of a sudden but gradually, so that portions of the earlier organizations always persist alongside the more recent one, and even in normal development transformation is never complete and residues of earlier fixations may still be retained in the final configuration. (pp. 228–29)

This passage clarifies Freud's recurrent practice of finding similarity-in-difference rather than mutual exclusion among psychic phenomena. It also serves as a gloss on much of Freud's linguistic undertaking itself, the purpose of which is to bypass the limitations of an incomplete science and to escape from the confines of the lexicon, whose more or less fixed and univocal meanings are not adequate to the processive aspects of psychic life. Thus Freud crafted an expression that tends toward the poetic; it is resonant; it blends or fuses different realms of experience; and, in its inclusive thrust, it dialectically returns upon itself, interacting with previous meanings and anticipating others. The interaction in and among the apparent verbal antitheses also constitutes on the strictly lexical level a mimesis of the essay's dual theme—endingness and unendingness.

The drastic changes—personal, professional, and societal—that Freud finally lived through variously determined not only the theme and tone but also the nature of the writing in his late essay. In accord with the note of unendingness in its title, Freud preferred a genetic to a dogmatic discourse; the latter he found more apt for writing a complete and self-contained systematics. In the genetic discourse of "Analysis Terminable and Interminable," the most impressive element is not the grand organizational pattern but the lesser pattern of lexicality. Just as in Katharina's case history, we meet with a wealth of suggestive verbal usage, including instances of more abundant analogical dispersion (which is a kind of centrifugal movement). But opposed to the centrifugal movement prevailing in the vertical references and other lexical features of Katharina's case history, we encounter in this essay a distinctive centripetal movement as well. Accordingly, among the various modifications affecting the antitheses between lexical pairs is a tendency to narrow or collapse difference: what previously was separated tends toward unification. At this point, brief reflection leads us to realize that unification occurs in both the centrifugal and centripetal movements of Freud's lexicality. The unifying factor in a centripetal movement, however, is a counterforce to an initially posited

or implied antithesis—such a feature readily accommo-
dates to a critical, conceptual treatise in genetic discourse.
We must not conclude, however, that Freud collapsed antitheses only because he had reflected rationally on them;
there was also a contribution to rapprochements from his
imagination, which was wont to draw analogies between
the most diverse phenomena and to bring them into the
nearness of a fantasied present (Mahony 1986).

Clearly, the different kinds of unification exemplied in
Freud's two polar texts represent a quintessential element
in his discourse. If his prose of solidarity and nonapartheid
obtains in both the imaginative narrative and the conceptual treatise, the effects of unification are yet more remarkable in the latter—like the Scholastic philosophers, Freud
could well have said, *"Distinguo ut uniam"* (I distinguish in
order to unite).

Postlude

Freud's writings are frequently classified according to subject and genre. Strachey's subject classifications are quite familiar: anthropology, mythology and history of religion; art, literature, and the theory of aesthetics; dreams; general psychological theory; the technique of psychoanalysis and the theory of psychotherapy; and so forth. In terms of genre, Freud's works may be divided into theoretical essays, history, dialogues, autobiography, letters, and so on. A more dynamic classification, first suggested by Freud himself, would arrange works according to the prevalence of dogmatic or genetic style. In dogmatic discourse, the mode of initial conception and the mode of scriptive presentation ordinarily diverge markedly; there is less such divergence in genetic discourse, especially in Freud's private genetic discourse. Alerting ourselves to this very discursive procedure that was favored by Freud, we have perceived significant similarities in two works that superficially seem very different.

A cardinal feature of Freud's genetic discourse is its use of a resonant language for scientific ends. Freud at his best (as he often was) wrote with a third hand and ear, responsive to unconscious processes, whose displacement and condensation led him to discern unifying patterns in the most diverse data. His writing described as well as enacted unconscious mechanisms, and like the good patient, Freud the writer both observed and participated in the analytic process. Yet however prominent were his capacities for observation and participation, they were surpassed by his linguistic achievement. As Eissler rightly said: Freud's "power to observe, to judge, to draw inferences—indispensable as they were to the greatness of his work . . . have to take a secondary place to the genius of his language" (Eissler 1977, p. 277).

Freud enlisted his rare linguistic power to convey a vision of life of impressive range. In this he reminds us of such classic writers as Virgil, Dante, Shakespeare, Cervantes, and Goethe. All these writers examine the whole field of human activity and the complete gamut of human emotions and let us participate in their incredible vitality, endurance, and heroic commitment to the human cause. To read these writers, including Freud, is to deepen our understanding of our own humanity, to realize our potential stature, and to increase our awareness of the endless complexity of history and our place in it. Faults Freud surely had, but however short he fell of his own ideals, he would agree with Goethe that "the first and last task of genius is the love of truth." Accordingly, he helped make worthy of serious scientific investigation that dreaming part of us that had previously been so contemptuously dismissed from the court of sober consideration. What is more, he gave a new, exalted context to our animal side: "The highest and the lowest are always closest to each other in the sphere of sexuality" (Freud 1905b, pp. 161–62). And immediately he went on to quote from *Faust:* "Vom Himmel durch die Welt zur Hölle" ('from heaven through the world to hell'). As Freud was wont to repeat, in their ready juxtaposition of opposites, the productions of the unconscious are truly witty.

Freud's personality enabled him to be quite at home with wit, both in perceiving it and in using it. We may remind ourselves of his remark that a patient's ability to make jokes points to a change toward the domination of his ego. Franz Alexander tells us that on informal occasions, Freud "propounded the most significant ideas in a light conversational, casual tone. He liked to illustrate a point with anecdotes and jokes, was an excellent raconteur, and even serious topics were robbed of the artificial austerity with which they are so frequently invested" (Alexander 1940). Such an observation has deeper implications when we relate it to Freud's understanding of the joke. Whereas a dream is dreamt in order not to be understood, a joke requires its own intelligibility; dreams and jokes are respectively the most asocial and the most social forms of discourse (Freud 1905c, p. 179). Bearing this in mind, we may say that Freud strives to compose an eminently intelligible social discourse, diametrically opposed to neurosis, which he repeatedly characterizes as asocial (Freud 1913, pp. 73–74, 159; 1919, p. 261). Freud's style is jokelike; the style of Jacques Lacan, because of his own deliberate strategy to avoid facile comprehension, tends toward dreamlike.

Pursuing Freud's notion that a joke is developed play, we can further characterize his style. He had "basically an ironic mind" (Eissler 1965, p. 390; see also Schur 1972, pp. 429 and n), and like all ironists he hated illusion. More precisely, Freud was a master of what is called romantic irony, whereby one has an acute self-reflective awareness of the elusiveness of knowledge and one attempts to rise above that limitation through simultaneous detachment and commitment (Muecke 1969). As we have seen, Freud can maintain a free critical detachment toward himself, the object of investigation, the linguistic means of communicating his investigative results, and the audience—all the while being involved in fostering the essentially positive spirit of romantic irony.

It is precisely in genetic discourse that we best see Freud in his role as romantic ironist. Assuming both commitment and detachment and aided by a playful, evocative language, he changes direction with ease, from self-humor to ponderous theme to impressive example, and so adroitly on. His composition blends both work and imagination, the weighty and the light. I know that I may jolt my readers if I say that Freud's genetic writing is also festive and celebratory, but I hold to the literal fullness of that claim. Freud's genetic discourse not only describes unconscious processes but also can enact and dominate them. Like the *fort/da* game of his grandson but on a grander scale, Freud's genetic style throughout his career is that of a conquistadorial master.

I consider erroneous and superficial any cavalier dismissal of the discursive aspects of Freud's writing on the grounds that such a preoccupation is "merely aesthetic."

For the psychodynamics and aesthetics of Freud's discourse are not mutually exclusive. More and more recognition is being rightly given to the critical place of style in a broad range of disciplines—ethnography, philosophy, sociology, and history. A recent remark by an eminent historian is pertinent to my position: "With a return of historians' attention to the discursive aspects of their enterprise," White writes, "they are now put in a position of having to recognize that imagination may have as much a role in the production of 'knowledge' as it was formerly thought to have only in the production of 'fine writing' which distinguishes historians with 'style' from their less 'interesting' colleagues" (Hayden White 1986, pp. 109–10). A similar thesis runs through Geertz's (1988) fascinating survey of anthropological literature.

How, then, should we read Freud? To begin an answer, I shall return to Strachey's translation, which, like all translations, is an interpretive reading. Following Ornston, I have pointed out how verbal networks in the Rat Man case were undone in the English translation (Ornston 1982, 1985; Mahony 1986). I would now even venture to say that the unitary design and implicative verbal force in Freud's subtext were defensively undone by Strachey in part because of the ideological compartmentalizations inherent in Strachey's sociological and scientific attitudes. In stripping away Freud's affect, Strachey's translation gives evidence of defensive isolation, and its suppression of perceived defects in the original text might well have arisen in part from repression and defensive idealization. In brief, to read Freud, one needs to be aware of the distortions in Strachey's translation.

The manifold intricacy of Freud's texts must be approached with reading skills equal to the challenge. If one presumes that Freud's texts are dogmatically self-sufficient and complete, one is starting with an enormous handicap and may never arrive at the point of integrating into one's reading the hermeneutics of suspicion that Freud, along with Nietzsche and Marx, contributed to modern culture. My own approach presumes that Freud's texts, like crystals, have fault lines, and I wonder where they are and how wittingly as well as unwittingly they are covered up. I muse about whether Freud's self-irony fully accounts for the gaps or contradictions in his report. Given the foiling nature of the unconscious, these questions are where I begin, not end, my enquiry. In addition, by splitting my ego into participant and observer roles, I aim to respond antiphonally to the dual activity that characterized Freud's own compositional creativity. Said somewhat differently, critics are likely these days to speak of an analytic space, but we must also think about a writing space and a reading space.

As readers we must also carefully follow the course of Freud's thought, word by word, sentence by sentence (Sachs 1945, pp. 98–99; Sterba 1982, p. 86). We must also, as the text warrants, analyze our transference to Freud. For clarification of this point, I shall bring in a blunder in Strachey's translation of "Analysis Terminable and Interminable" which I have refrained from mentioning up to now. Rendering *ungestillten* as "appeased" instead of "unappeased," Strachey has Freud say: "the appeased wish for a penis is destined to be converted into a wish for a baby and for a husband, who possesses a penis" (97/251). The fact that this nonsequitur has been overlooked by countless readers testifies, I think, to Freud's authorial power.

Freud himself points to three different kinds of readers in "Analysis Terminable and Interminable": the skeptical, the optimistic, and the ambitious (p. 223). Of course, the different kinds of readers, like analysis, are unending. Nevertheless, the specificity of a psychoanalytic reading of Freud demands analysis of one's transference to him. And depending on the text, the reader should analyze his transferences to Freud's patients as well as to the constructions of incompetent and ideal readers that Freud himself proposes. These tasks lead us to realize that a genuine psychoanalytic reading, like analysis itself, is unending and ultimately indeterminate. We should be ready to readjust our perspectives as we move through Freud's text (by reconstituting our interpretative acts, we even participate in the creation of the text, especially the processive kind). In other words, we must be willing to construct, or better yet, reconstruct with Freud the writer, much as Alexander reported he did in conversing with Freud: "To a suggestion he would respond with a question or with a "perhaps," spinning the idea further and waiting for the other to take up the thread again and offer some new suggestion. One had the feeling that one and Freud were working out something together" (Alexander 1940).

And if, as I said, there is a festal element in Freud's prose, we must be prepared to perform a celebratory reading, in its own way analogous to Freud's followers' celebrating his *Totem and Taboo* by treating him to a dinner that they hailed as a "totemic festival" (Mahony 1987). Such a possibility also behooves us to heed Freud's paradigmatic directives about a desirably playful and concomitantly responsible reading of *Civilization and Its Discontents:* "I wrote the book with purely analytic intentions," he

insisted, "based on my former existence as an analytic writer, in brooding contemplation, concerned to promote the
concept of the feeling of guilt to its very end. The feeling of
guilt is created by the renunciation of aggression. Now it's
up to you to play with this idea" (Sterba 1982, p. 116).

An assured answer to the question what kind of reading Freud prescribes is that such a reading has no end. The
explorable wonder of his texts is as vast as the universe he
discovered within us—with its own peculiar fields of attrac-
tion, meteors, comets, constellations, and galaxies. Our
wonderment leaps beyond its former bounds, I suggest, if
we bring within its scope the uncanny conjunction, inex-
haustible in myth, that the word *galaxy* is rooted in the
Greek for "milk" . . .

References

Alexander, F. (1940). Recollections of Berggasse 19. *Psy-choanal. Quart. 9*, 195–204.

Anzieu, D. (1975). *L'Auto-analyse de Freud et la découverte de la psychanalyse,* vol. 1. Paris: Presses Universitaires de France.

———. (1987). Some alterations of the ego which makes analyses interminable. *Internat. J. Psycho-Anal. 68*, 9–20.

Argelander, H. (1976). Im Sprechstunden-Interview bei Freud: technische Überlegungen zu Freuds Fall "Katharina." *Psyche 30*, 665–702.

———. (1978). Das psychoanalytische Erstinterview und seine Methode: ein Nachtrag zu Freuds Fall Katharina. *Psyche 32*, 1089–98.

Arlow, J. (1987). Perspectives on Freud's 'Analysis terminable and interminable.' In J. Sandler, ed., *On Freud's 'Analysis Terminable and Interminable,'* pp. 73–88. London: Internat. Psychoanal. Assn.

Bacon, F. (1623). *De Dignitate et Augmentis Scientiarum (Liber Sextus).* In J. Spedding, R. Ellis, and D. Heath, eds., *The Works of Francis Bacon.* London, 1861.

Benedikt, M. (1906). *Aus meinem Leben: Erinnerungen und Erörterungen*. Vienna: Carl Konegen.

Berenstein, I. (1987). Analysis terminable and interminable, fifty years on. *Internat. J. Psycho-Anal. 68*, 21–36.

Bernfeld, S.(1944). Freud's earliest theories and the School of Helmholtz. *Psychoanal. Quart.* 13, 341–62.

Bertin, C. (1987). *Marie Bonaparte: A Life*. New Haven: Yale University Press.

Blum, H. (1987). Analysis terminable and interminable: A half century perspective. *Internat. J. Psychoanal. 68*, 37–48.

Bonaparte, M. (1936). *Topsy: Chow-Chow au poil d'or*. Paris: Editions Denoël et Steele.

Brücke, T. (1928). *Ernst Brücke*. Vienna: Julius Sprenger.

Clark, R. (1980). *Freud: The Man and the Cause*. New York: Random House.

Cooper, A. (1987). Comments on Freud's 'Analysis terminable and interminable.' In J. Sandler, ed., *On Freud's 'Analysis Terminable and Interminable,'* pp. 127–48. London: Internat. Psychoanal. Assn.

Eissler, K. (1965). *Medical Orthodoxy and the Future of Psychoanalysis*. New York: International Universities Press.

———. (1971). *Talent and Genius*. New York: Quadrangle Books.

Ellenberger, H. (1970). *The Discovery of the Unconscious*. New York: Basic Books.

Fichtner, G., and Hirschmüller, A. (1985). Freuds "Katharina": Hintergrund, Enstehungsgeschichte und Bedeutung einer frühen psychoanalytischen Krankengeschichte. *Psyche 39*, 220–40.

Freud, A. (1980). Foreword to *Topsy* by Marie Bonaparte. In *The Writings of Anna Freud*, vol. 8, pp. 358–61. New York: International Universities Press, 1981.

Freud, S. (1940–68). *Gesammelte Werke*. 18 vols. Frankfurt-am-Main: Fischer-Verlag.

———. (1953–74). *The Standard Edition of the Complete*

Psychological Works, ed. and trans. J. Strachey. 24 vols. London: Hogarth. All the following references to this edition (*SE*) are by volume and page.

_____. (1892–94). Extracts from Freud's footnotes to his translation of Charcot's *Tuesday Lectures. SE,* 1:137–41.

_____. (1893). Charcot. *SE,* 3:11–23.

_____. (1893–95). *Studies on Hysteria. SE,* vol. 2; *GW,* 1:75–313.

_____. (1894). The neuro-psychoses of defence. *SE,* 3:43–61.

_____. (1895). On the grounds for detaching a particular syndrome from neurasthenia under the description 'anxiety neurosis.' *SE,* 3:90–115.

_____. (1896a). The aetiology of hysteria. *SE,* 3:189–221.

_____. (1896b). Further remarks on the neuro-psychoses of defence. *SE,* 3:162–85.

_____. (1900). *The Interpretation of Dreams. SE,* vols. 4–5.

_____. (1901). Autobiographical note. *SE.* 3:325.

_____. (1905a). Fragment of an analysis of a case of hysteria. *SE,* 7:7–122.

_____. (1905b). Three essays on sexuality. *SE,* 7:130–243.

_____. (1905c). *Jokes and Their Relation to the Unconscious. SE,* 8.

_____. (1909). Analysis of a phobia in a five-year-old boy. *SE,* 10:5–149.

_____. (1910a). Five lectures on psycho-analysis. *SE,* 11:9–55.

_____. (1910b). The future prospects of psycho-analytic therapy. *SE,* 11:141–51.

_____. (1913). *Totem and Taboo. SE,* vol. 13.

_____. (1915–17). *Introductory Lectures on Psycho-analysis. SE,* vols. 16–17.

_____. (1919). Preface to Reik's *Ritual: Psychoanalytic Studies. SE,* 17:259–63.

_____. (1920). The psychogenesis of a case of homosexuality in a woman. *SE,* 18:147–72.

_____. (1925). An autobiographical study. *SE,* 20:3–74.

——. (1926). The question of lay analysis. *SE*, 20:183–258.

——. (1933). New introductory lectures on psycho-analysis. *SE*, 22:3–182; *GW*, vol. 15.

——. (1937). Analysis terminable and interminable. *SE*, 23:216–254; *GW*, 16:59–99.

——. (1940a). An outline of psycho-analysis. *SE*, 23:144–207; *GW*, 17:63–138. Also in *Internationale Zeitschrift für Psychoanalyse 25* (1940): 7–67.

——. (1940b). Some elementary lessons in psycho-analysis. *SE*, 23:281–86; *GW*, 17:141–47.

——. (1940–1941). Letter to Josef Breuer. *SE*, 1:147–48.

——. (1956). Report of my studies in Paris and Berlin. *SE*, 1:5–15.

——. (1960). *Letters of Sigmund Freud: 1873–1939*, E. Freud. London: Hogarth Press.

——. (1963). *Psychoanalysis and Faith*, Ed. H. Meng and E. Freud; trans. E. Mosbacher. London: Hogarth.

——. (1966). *Sigmund Freud and Lou Andreas-Salomé: Letters*, ed. E. Pfeiffer. New York: Harcourt Brace.

——. (1970). *The Letters of Sigmund Freud and Arnold Zweig*, ed. E. Freud. New York: Harcourt Brace.

——. (1974). *The Freud/Jung Letters*, ed. W. McGuire; trans. R. Manheim and R. Hull. Princeton: Princeton University Press. Translation of *Briefwechsel (1906–1916)*, ed. W. McGuire and W. Sauerländer. Frankfurt am Main: S. Fischer Verlag, 1974.

——. (1985). *The Complete Letters of Sigmund Freud to Wilhelm Fliess (1887–1904)*, ed. and trans. J. Masson. Cambridge: Harvard University Press.

Geertz, C. (1988). *Works and Lives: The Anthropologist as Author*. Palo Alto: Stanford University Press.

Glenn, J. (1980). Freud's adolescent patients: Katharina, Dora and the "homosexual woman." In M. Kanzer and J. Glenn, eds., *Freud and His Patients*, pp. 23–47. New York: Jason Aronson.

Guillain, G. (1955). *J.-M. Charcot: Sa vie, son oeuvre.* Paris: Masson.

Jaques, E. (1982). *The Form of Time.* New York: Crane Russak.

Jones, E. (1953–57). *The Life and Work of Sigmund Freud,* vols. 1–3. New York: Basic Books.

Junker, H. Unpubl. Ms. On reading Freud: Comments on "Analysis Terminable and Interminable."

Knoepfmacher, H. (1979). Sigmund Freud and the B'nai B'rith. *J. Amer. Psychoanal. Assn. 27,* 441–50.

Leupold-Löwenthal, H. (1987). Notes on Sigmund's 'Analysis terminable and interminable.' In J. Sandler, ed., *On Freud's 'Analysis Terminable and Interminable,'* pp. 47–72. London: Internat. Psychoanal. Assn.

Lieberman, J. (1985). *Acts of Will: The Life and Work of Otto Rank.* New York: Free Press.

Lyons, J. (1968). *Introduction to Theoretical Linguistics.* Cambridge: Cambridge University Press.

Mahony, P. (1979a). Friendship and its discontents. *Contemporary Psychoanalysis 15,* 55–109.

———. (1979b). The budding International Association of Psychoanalysis and its discontents. *Psychoanalysis and Contemporary Thought 2,* 551–92.

———. (1986). *Freud and the Rat Man.* New Haven: Yale University Press.

———. (1987). *Freud as a Writer,* rev. ed. New Haven: Yale University Press.

Meissner, W. (1979). Studies on hysteria—Katharina. *Psychoanal. Quart. 48,* 587–600.

Muecke, D. (1969). *The Compass of Irony.* London: Methuen.

Nunberg, H., and Federn, E., eds. (1967–75). *Minutes of the Vienna Psychoanalytic Society,* vols. 2, 4. New York: International Universities Press.

Ornston, D. (1982). Strachey's influence. *Internat. J. Psycho-Anal. 63,* 409–26.

———. (1985). Freud's conception is different from Strachey's. *J. Amer. Psychoanal. Assn.* 33, 337–70.

———. Unpubl. Ms. On revising the *Standard Edition* of Freud's writings.

Reiser, L. (1987). Topsy—Living and Dying: A Footnote to History. *Psychoanal. Quart.* 56, 667–88.

Rohner, L. (1966). *Der deutsche Essay.* Berlin: Hermann Luchterhand Verlag.

Romm, S. (1983). *The Unwelcome Intruder: Freud's Struggle with Cancer.* New York: Praeger Publishers.

Rose, G. (1980). *The Power of Form.* New York: International Universities Press.

Roudinesco, E. (1982). *La Bataille de cents ans: Histoire de la psychanalyse en France.* Paris: Editions Ramsay.

Sachs, H. (1945). *Freud: Master and Friend.* London: Imago.

Schafer, R. (1981). *Narrative Actions in Psychoanalysis.* Worcester, Mass.: Clark University Press.

Schönau, W. (1968). *Sigmund Freuds Prosa.* Stuggart: J. B. Metzlersche Verlag.

Schur, M. (1972). *Freud: Living and Dying.* New York: International Universities Press.

Sterba, R. (1982). *Reminiscences of a Viennese Psychoanalyst.* Detroit: Wayne State University Press.

Swales, P. (1988). Freud, Katharina, and the first "wild analysis." In P. Stepansky, ed., *Freud: Appraisals and Reappraisals,* vol. 3, pp. 81–164. Hillsdale, N.J.: Analytic Press.

White, H. (1986). Between science and symbol. *Times Literary Supplement,* January 31, pp. 109–10.

Index